Towards a Cornish Philosophy

Other Cornish books from Evertype

Gwerryans an Planettys (H. G. Wells, tr. Nicholas Williams 2013)

Ky Teylu Baskerville (Arthur Conan Doyle, tr. Nicholas Williams 2012)

Flehes an Hens Horn (Edith Nesbit, tr. Nicholas Williams 2012)

Phyllis in Piskie-land (J. Henry Harris 2012)

An Beybel Sans: The Holy Bible in Cornish (tr. Nicholas Williams 2011)

Whedhlow ha Drollys a Gernow Goth (Nigel Roberts, tr. Nicholas Williams 2011)

The Beast of Bodmin Moor: Best Goon Brèn (Alan Kent, tr. Neil Kennedy 2011)

Enys Tresour (Robert Louis Stevenson, tr. Nicholas Williams 2010)

Whedhlow Kernowek: Stories in Cornish (A.S.D. Smith, ed. Nicholas Williams 2010)

Henry Jenner's Handbook of the Cornish Language (ed. Michael Everson 2010)

The Cult of Relics: Devocyon dhe Greryow (Alan Kent, tr. Nicholas Williams, 2010)

Jowal Lethesow: Whedhel a'm West a Gernow
(Craig Weatherhill, tr. Nicholas Williams, 2009)

Skeul an Tavas: A coursebook in Standard Cornish (Ray Chubb, 2009)

Kensa Lyver Redya
(Harriette Treadwell & Margaret Free, tr. Eddie Foirbeis Climo, 2009)

Adro dhe'n Bÿs in Peswar Ugans Dëdh
(Jules Verne, abridged and tr. Kaspar Hocking, 2009)

A Concise Dictionary of Cornish Place-Names (Craig Weatherhill, 2009)

Alys in Pow an Anethow (Lewis Carroll, tr. Nicholas Williams, 2009)

Form and Content in Revived Cornish
(Everson, Weatherhill, Chubb, Deacon, Williams, 2006)

Towards Authentic Cornish (Nicholas Williams, 2006)

Writings on Revived Cornish (Nicholas Williams, 2006)

Cornish Today (Nicholas Williams, 2006)

Towards a Cornish Philosophy

Values, Thought, and Language for the
West Britons in the Twenty-First Century

Alan M. Kent

evertype

2013

Published by Evertype, Cnoc Sceichín, Leac an Anfa, Cathair na Mart, Co. Mhaigh Eo, Éire. *www.evertype.com.*

Text © 2013 Alan M. Kent.
Preface © 2013 Mathew Staunton.

First edition 2013.

A catalogue record for this book is available from the British Library.

ISBN-10 1-78201-045-9
ISBN-13 978-1-78201-045-6

Edited by Mathew Staunton.

Typeset in Baskerville by Michael Everson.

Cover design by Michael Everson.

Printed and bound by LightningSource.

Contents

Preface

Timely Reflections on Cornish Philisophy

Like Ireland and Scotland, Cornwall became a popular tourist destination for well-to-do English families during the Napoleonic Wars. Forced to abandon their usual itineraries in France and Italy by the Little Corporal's continental campaigns, these genteel thrill-seekers turned instead to the unfashionable fringes of their own Kingdom. Publishers were quick to take advantage of the situation and provide maps and guidebooks for these clueless holidaymakers. The literature they produced depicted Cornwall as a wild and wonderful place, full of ivy-covered ruins, mysterious stones, and sublime landscapes. The colourful characters who peopled this land were straight out of the Gothic novels that were all the rage at the time. They were dark and brooding, mere extensions of the landscapes they lived in, utterly at one with their environment, and as different to the average Londoner as chalk and cheddar cheese.

This fantastic place was as much a literary construction as the novelesque imagery that has been mapped onto it since the second half of the Georgian era. The perception of Cornishness that developed outside Cornwall during his period has, nonetheless, proved resilient and visitors still tend to view the sights through romantic spectacles manufactured more than a century ago. The products of this external gaze have been examined by academics across various fields but the picture that emerges is far from complete. Apart from the opinions of a handful of Cornish nationalists (the traditional subject matter of historians and political scientists), we learn little of the worldview of the Cornish themselves. How have they perceived themselves and their relationship with their territory throughout the ages? How have they attempted to understand themselves? Is there any evidence of a native Cornish philosophy? Researchers in the field of Celtic Studies, predominantly concerned with the cultures of Ireland and Scotland, have not yet provided satisfactory answers to these questions.

In the monograph that follows, Dr Alan M. Kent aims to identify the contours of this gap and assemble the tools necessary for filling it. His is not the exhaustive study of Cornish philosophy he calls for in his preliminary statements, nor does he claim to provide answers to the many questions he poses throughout. Rather, this is a vitally important first step along the network of paths that lead to an understanding of this neglected subject and one that leaves us with clearer and more pertinent questions and objectives.

Throughout his book, Dr Kent deftly draws our attention to threshold moments in the evolution of Cornish thinking. He finds tantalizing traces of a native worldview in the earliest Cornish-language texts, and compares the writings of Nicholas Roscarrock and Richard Carew to reveal a shift from Medieval to Renaissance frames of reference. He looks for indications of a specifically Cornish perspective on life in the relationship of the Cornish to language and the geology of their environment. More importantly, however, he identifies the outlines of a uniquely Cornish philosophy in the ideological space where the Enlightenment overlaps with Romanticism. Reframing the "Cornish paradox", he argues that Cornishness cannot be reduced to one or other of the traditional binary opposites (imagination—pragmatism, emotion—reason) applied to

Cornwall and its people by generations of academics, writers, and nationalists. We must instead begin to see the Cornish worldview as a subtle blend of Western philosophies and local modes of thought developed over centuries, and apply ourselves to unpicking its various strands using all of the methodologies at our disposal.

Towards a Cornish Philosophy is a timely and important book and one that will inform research on Cornish philosophy in the future.

Dr Mathew D. Staunton
Oxford, August 2013

Acknowledgements

I would like to extend my thanks to Allen E. Ivey, Craig Weatherhill, Loic Rich, Ken George, James Whetter, Duncan Yeates, Neil Kennedy, and Jim Pengelly in their help in the preparation of this monograph.

Alan M. Kent
Probus, August 2013

1

Philosophy in Cornish Studies and in Celtic Studies

In Cornu-English, when contemplating if a particular issue is really of concern to him or her, the Cornish person might decide that it may not be relevant or urgent—and there responds with "*Matter, do ut?*" We know that, since the inception of Cornish Studies, the issue of Cornish philosophy has suffered considerable neglect. This monograph questions whether or not it matters to us. There are many definitions of philosophy but, put simply, it can be seen as a field in which humanity investigates problems connected with reality and existence. In so doing, it investigates values, knowledge, and thought—and generally examines these by exploring concepts of reason and language. Although such topics are of interest to other fields, philosophy generally conducts its examination through rational argument and has an interest in developing systematic approaches to this investigation. Philosophy, therefore, ought to be of interest to those pursuing Cornish Studies, because, by definition, the field involves an examination of the most basic beliefs, attitudes, and concepts belonging to both individuals and groups. If we are to regard individuals as "Cornish", and to recognize the socio-geographic group as being Cornish, then it stands to reason that we should be interested in those basic beliefs, attitudes, and concepts belonging to them.[1]

---

1   J. Gillespie (ed.), *Our Cornwall: The Stories of Cornish Men and Women*

In the recent past, such an examination has been conducted by a number of scholars interested in understanding what makes the Cornish exist as both an historical group and continue to self-define in all kinds of areas of contemporary human activity.[2] The field of Cornish Studies has, thus, been more than willing to embrace the academic treatment of identity (itself an important aspect of Cornishness) and so-called "identity theory",[3] but has been less confident in embracing philosophical enquiry. This is a curious defect considering the widespread interest in Cornish values and problems; not to mention long-term enquiry into language (both the revival of the Cornish language[4] and the use of Cornu-English[5]). This monograph, therefore, offers an initial corrective.

Why has this happened? Certainly, the issue has a lot to do with the origins of Cornish Studies itself. As documented

---

(Padstow, 1988); J. Angarrack, *Our Future is History: Identity, Law and the Cornish Question* (Bodmin, 2002); B. Deacon, S. Schwartz and D. Holman, *The Cornish Family: The Roots of Our Future*, (Fowey, 2004).

2. See, for example. M. W. Tschirschky, *Die Erfindung der Kertischen Nation Cornwall: Kultur, Identität und ethnischer Nationalismus in der Britischen Periphere* (Heidelburg, 2006).

3 J. Willett, "Cornish Identity: Vague Notion or Social Fact?" in P. Payton (ed.),*Cornish Studies: Sixteen* (Exeter, 2008), pp. 183-205; R. Dickinson, "Meanings of Cornishness: A Study of Contemporary Cornish Identity" in P. Payton (ed.), *Cornish Studies: Eighteen* (Exeter, 2010), pp. 70-100; Stuart Dunmore, "Xians or Yish? Language attitudes and cultural identities on Britain's Celtic Periphery" in P. Payton (ed.), *Cornish Studies: Nineteen* (Exeter, 2011), pp. 60-83.

4 See P. Payton and B. Deacon, "The Ideology of language Revival" in P. Payton (ed.), *Cornwall Since the War: The Contemporary History of a European Region* (Redruth, 1993), pp. 271-90; P. Dunbar and K. George, *Cornish for the Twenty-First Century* (Cornwall, 1997); M. Everson, C. Weatherhill, R. Chubb, B. Deacon and N. Williams, *Form and Content in Revived Cornish* (Westport, 2007).

5 See K. C. Phillipps, *A Glossary of Cornish Dialect* (Padstow, 1993); A. M. Kent, "Bringin' the Dunkey down from the Carn: Cornu-English in Context 1549-2005—A Provisional Analysis" in H. L. C. Tristram

elsewhere by several commentators, modern Cornish Studies has its origins in three fields: local history, antiquarianism, and archaeology.[6] Although researchers in these fields have sometimes "accidentally" touched on issues of philosophy, there was never any direct engagement.[7] Herein we notice a major difficulty to be overcome: philosophy has sometimes been viewed as too ethereal or theoretical for Cornish Studies; it being a topic not readily associated with historical or even contemporary Cornwall. Indeed, for some observers the very notion that a comparatively small territory such as Cornwall could facilitate the evolution of a distinctive philosophy might appear unfeasible or absurd.

Over the past twenty years, however, Cornish Studies has engaged more readily with new fields and expanded the topics suitable for enquiry. There have been debates over differing philosophies of language reinvigoration, literary enquiry, the place and purpose of the Cornish Revival, and the nature of Cornish Studies itself, which have touched on material connected to philosophy. Indeed, two of modern Cornish Studies' main architects—Bernard Deacon and Philip Payton—have developed research along these lines.[8] The difficulty has been that philosophy is often perceived as disconnected from working-class people's lives. It is the stuff of the high-blown, the pinnacle of the academy. Philosophy might

(ed.), *The Celtic Englishes IV* (Potsdam, 2005), pp.6-33; L. Merton (ed.), *Thus Es Et: An Anthology of Cornish Dialect* (London, 2011).

6   See P. Payton, "Cornwall in Context: The New Cornish Historiography" in P. Payton (ed.), *Cornish Studies: Five* (Exeter, 1997), pp.9-20; B. Deacon, "From 'Cornish Studies' to 'Critical Cornish Studies': Reflections on Methodology" in Payton, op.cit. (2004), pp.13-29.

7   See C. Thomas (ed.), *Cornish Studies / Studhyansow Kernewek 1- 15* (Redruth, 1973-1987).

8   See Payton, op.cit.; Deacon, op.cit.. See also P. Payton, *A Vision of Cornwall* (Fowey, 2002); B. Deacon, *Cornwall: A Concise History* (Cardiff, 2007).

also seem peripheral to the concerns of traditional topics within Cornish Studies—those of mining, fishing, agriculture, emigration, and politics. Academics are constantly being told that their research must have relevance and real outcomes, and that impact must be assessed. Although one could argue that philosophy rarely touches the lives of those outside of the academy, here I aim to show that it has had, and continues to have, a profound effect on the lives and identities of Cornish people. The time is now right to reflect on the evolution of native Cornish philosophy and examine its impact.

However, Cornish Studies can also be seen as part of a wider Celtic Studies. This is despite the fact that Cornwall has generally (until recently) been given short shrift in this field. Actually, Cornish Studies may have gained its energy from a greater awareness of European regional studies and, indeed, global interest in devolution and small nations. It must be noted, though, that the field of Celtic Studies itself has also, for the most part, failed to embrace the subject of philosophical enquiry. This lacuna is evident in John T. Koch's comprehensive five-volume *Celtic Culture: A Historical Encyclopedia* (2006) where, among hundreds of separate entries, philosophy is not included.[9] As in Cornish Studies, the field tends to be touched upon in other more easily distinguishable entries on history, language, culture, and revival, or by the focus on philosophical concerns in literature.

In general, Celtic Studies has tended to align itself to the concerns of Celtic Spirituality, a convenient holdall including several often conflicting philosophical elements—some secular, some Christian, some Celto-Christian, some Pagan, and some Neo-Pagan.[10] Concepts such as "words of wisdom" and

9   J. T. Koch (ed.), *Celtic Culture: A Historical Encyclopedia* (Santa Barbara and Oxford, 2006).

10   Some of the more important contributions here include S. Toulson. *The Celtic Christianity: A Reminder of the Christianity we Lost* (London, 1987);

"inspiration" tend to be used alongside these quasi-philo-sophical texts.[11] The reader will note that these elements are more often concerned with religious philosophy than with other branches of philosophy. They have come to popularly represent a great deal about the Celtic world-view and philosophy, and occupy a considerable amount of shelf space in bookshops. Often, the philosophical intent of the original text is taken out of context and is redefined for what Bowman has usefully labelled "Cardiac Celts".[12] Contributors to Koch's encyclopaedia tend to have a better engagement with ancient philosophers and their views of Celtic peoples, though this is dealt with on a piecemeal basis.[13] The Celtic worlds discussed are those of ancient Europe rather than the present-day peoples of Britain, Ireland, and Brittany.

As we might expect, interest in philosophical issues from the smaller Celtic territories such as Cornwall and the Isle of Man are virtually non-existent,[14] with only a tokenistic consideration of Brittany. This is the struggle of a minority culture striving to be heard within the field of Celtic Studies and its predominantly English-language academic mode of enquiry. Wales and Scotland generally receive more attention, though philosophy is again only really examined as a tangent from

W. P. Marsh and C. Bamford (eds.), *Celtic Christianity: Ecology and Holiness—An Anthology* (Edinburgh,. 1986); N. Pennick, *Celtic Sacred Landscapes* (London, 1996).

11 See, for example. E. Gill and D. Everett (eds.), *Celtic Verse: An Inspirational Anthology of Poems, Prose, Prayers. and Words of Wisdom* (London, 1998); S. Heinz, *Celtic Symbols* (London and New York, 1999); L. Kergoat (ed. and tr.), *Proverbes Bretons* (Kerangwenn, 1998).

12 M. Bowman, "Cardiac Celts: Images of Celts in Paganism" in G. Harvey and C. Hardman (eds.), *Paganism Today* (London, 1995), pp.242-51.

13 Koch. op.cit.

14. A few philosophical questions are raised in texts contained in A. M. Kent and T. Saunders (eds. and tars.), *Looking at the Mermaid: A Reader in Cornish Literature 900-1900* (London, 2000), and in R. C. Creswell

other entries. We are aware, however, that both of these territories have a recognisable history of academic engagement with native and wider philosophy, as seen in the writings of Williams, Dix, and Sandry on Wales,[15] and Broadie and Henry on Scotland.[16] Like Cornwall, Wales still does not have enough ideological energy to form the level of philosophical engagement of Scotland. Clearly, the latter territory (larger and perhaps more assured of its cultural integrity) has more readily engaged with this aspect of its history.

The one exception is, perhaps, Ireland/Éire (a large nation-state) which seems to have enough clout to explore notions of philosophy in its history, its ancient and medieval literature, and issues affecting it in the current era. In historical writing, this can be seen in well-known, populist works such as Thomas Cahill's *How the Irish Saved Civilisation: The Untold Story of Ireland's Heroic Role from the Fall of Rome to the Rise of Medieval Europe* (1998) which sets a Europe-wide agenda to philosophizing about the significance of Irish culture and thought.[17] In literature, such a philosophical angle can be seen in what Minahane has labelled the "Christian Druids" or rather the *filid* or "philosopher poets" of the fifth century CE.[18] Kearney, meanwhile, has demonstrated in the context of Irish-British relations and what

(ed. and tr.) *Manannan's Cloak: An Anthology of Manx Literature* (London,. 2010).

15   D. Williams (ed.), *Raymond Williams: Who Speaks for Wales? Nation. Culture, Identity* (Cardiff, 2008); H. Dix, *After Raymond Williams: Cultural Materialism and the Break-Up of Britain* (Cardiff, 2008); A. Sandry, *Plaid Cymru: An Ideological Analysis*, (Cardiff, 2011).

16   A. Broadie (ed.), *The Cambridge Companion to the Scottish Enlightenment* (Cambridge, 2003), *A History of Scottish Philosophy* (Edinburgh, 2010); L. Henry, *Scottish Philosophy in its National Development* (Stockbridge, USA, 2013).

17   T. Cahail, *How the Irish Saved Civilisation: The Untold Story of Ireland's Heroic Role from the Fall of Rome to the Rise of Medieval Europe* (London, 1998)

18   J. Minahane, *The Christian Druids: On the filid or philosopher poets of Ireland* (Dublin, 1993).

he terms "sovereignty neurosis" how contemporary Ireland has had to negotiate its philosophical heritage between the competing demands of globalization and greater regional democracy.[19]

Two notable exceptions to all of this may be observed. Matthew Arnold's *On the Study of Celtic Literature* (1867) does examine some limited philosophical issues emanating out of his cross-cultural observations.[20] In short, Arnold believed that the Celtic peoples of Europe had assembled an interesting and significant literary heritage, but was guarded as to giving them the opportunity to run their own affairs. That said, Arnold did recognize a distinctive Celtic literary-philosophical approach. Meanwhile, Herbert Moore's *A Short History of Celtic Philosophy* (1920) attempted to draw connections between classical philosophy, druidry, and what we might term a "Celtic state of mind", yet his observations were primarily concerned with Ireland alone, with only a few diversions to Scotland and Wales.[21] Unsurprisingly, Cornwall, Brittany, and the Isle of Man are ignored.

19   R. Kearney, *Postnationalist Ireland: Politics, Culture, Philosophy* (London, 1997).

20   M. Arnold, *On the Study of Celtic Literature* (Charleston, South Carolina, n.d. [1867]). Cf. J. D. Wilson (ed.), *Matthew Arnold: Culture and Anarchy,* (Cambridge, 1932).

21   H. Moore, *A Short History of Celtic Philosophy* (Edinburgh and London, 1920).

2

Philosophy in Context

The apparent neglect of philosophy in Cornish Studies and Celtic Studies does not mean that it does not exist. Rather, it means that, as yet, it is an unploughed field. In order to tackle this neglect, it is necessary for us to understand philosophy in context and negotiate aspects of its contribution to native Cornish philosophies.

One important branch of philosophy is epistemology which is concerned with the nature and scope of existing knowledge. Here we are concerned with notions of belief and truth, and understanding the relationship between the two.[22] In the case of the Cornish, there may well be a certain set of beliefs about them, who they are, and what they do, but this does not necessarily represent the truth about them.[23] Indeed, the truth may be difficult to locate considering variety across the territory—from, say, west to east, north to south, or from a distinctive *Kernow* to those scattered across the globe. According to numerous philosophers of the past, such questions can only be solved by means of reason and rationalism. Logic is closely related to these two concepts and whilst some theorists believe

---

22 R. Audi, *Epistemology: A Contemporary Introduction to the Theory of Knowledge* (New York and London, 2010).

23 See, for example, W. H. Hudson, *The Land's End* (London, 1981 [1908]); M. Maclean, *The Literature of the Celts* (London, 1902). Cf. R. Lyon, *Cornwall's Historical Wars: A Brief Introduction* (Sheffield, 2012) and I. Arthurson, *The Perkin Warbeck Conspiracy* (Stroud, 1997).

in the power of logic as a tool,[24] it does not always follow that human behaviour is logical. For example, in the case of Cornwall, considering its early accommodation into the English nation state, the near destruction of its language, and its relatively small size,[25] logic would demand that it give up its quest for self-determination, devolution, or greater recognition.[26] However, quite possibly, in the early twenty-first century, the opposite is true. In this respect, Cornwall represents a particularly interesting case study for philosophy—since as well as issues of territory and identity, there are also important issues involving the philosophy of language, the philosophy of law (with particular relevance to the Stannary system[27]), the philosophy of religion, and questions of moral and political philosophy. This is not to mention the more esoteric aspects of philosophy such as metaphysics, which examines the relationship between the mind and body. Metaphysics also facilitates the group or the individual an understanding of their place in cosmology and in the existence of humanity as a whole. These are big questions, obviously, but important ones for the Cornish to come to terms with.

By nature, any understanding we have of native Cornish philosophies is bound to fit into the Western philosophical tradition. Despite geographical distance, these philosophies are bound—thanks to centuries of learning, scholarship, and the exchange of information—to have been influenced by ancient Graeco-Roman philosophy.[28] This philosophy leads

24   P. Tomassi, *Logic* (New York and London, 1999).

25   P. B. Ellis, *The Cornish Language and its Literature* (London, 1974).

26. Cf. P. B. Ellis, *The Celtic Revolution: A Study in Anti-Imperialism* (Talybont, 1985).

27   See G. Harrison, *Substance of a Report on the Laws and Jurisdiction of the Stannaries in Cornwall* (London, 1835); P. laity, T. Saunders and A.M. Kent, *The Reason Why: Cornwall's Status in Constitutional and International Law* (St Ives, 2001).

28   A. Kenny, *A New History of Western Philosophy* (Oxford, 2012).

inescapably to reflection on political systems, jurisdiction and justice, and wider philosophical investigation of the nature of comedy and tragedy, humour, and satire. However, for many centuries, from the Roman period to the Renaissance, it was the Christianization of that philosophy which dominated.[29] Certainly, it is these twin strands of Graeco-Roman thought and wider Christianization which are found in surviving literary texts with Cornish relevance from the post-Roman, Medieval, and Renaissance periods.[30] In the Renaissance period, many key thinkers began to view the Medieval age as one which was unsophisticated and even barbaric, and to seek new and modern ways of explaining and understanding the world.

In Cornwall, the difference between these philosophical approaches is best seen in the work of writers and thinkers such as Nicholas Roscarrock (c.1548–1634) and Richard Carew (1555–1620). Roscarrock, born in North Cornwall, was a Catholic and firmly committed to the achievement and centrality of the Saints, the Cornish language, and a sense of community on the western seaboard of Europe.[31] His was a philosophy born out of his Cornish heritage. Meanwhile, Carew, born at Antony in East Cornwall, embraced modernity and the English language, had a fruitful liaison with English culture, and viewed superstition and tradition sceptically.[32] These two positions are symbolic of the wider debate in Cornish philosophy that would take place over the next four hundred years and, to some degree, is still the focus of what it

29 See A. Phillips, *Re-claiming Cornwall's Celtic Christian Heritage* (Portreath, 2006).

30 See A. Le Braz, *Le Theatre Celtique* (Paris, 1905); B. Murdoch, *Cornish Literature* (Cambridge, 1993). J. T. Grimbert (ed.), *Tristan and Isolde: A Casebook* (New York and London, 1995).

31 N. Orme (ed.), *Nicholas Roscarrock's Lives of the Saints of Cornwall and Devon* (Exeter, 1992).

32 F.E. Halliday (ed.), *Richard Carew: The Survey of Cornwall* (London, 1953).

means to be Cornish today. Already in Carew we see his turn away from the Graeco-Roman philosophy of the past and the wider Christianization of Celtic culture which had occurred in Cornwall. Carew is significant, of course, because of his progressive thought, his use of logic and reasoning, and his embracing of the modern world. Generally, in other Celtic territories the older thought of the medieval period tended to last longer (because of their peripheral location, or the slower transfer of "Centralist" thought due to indigenous languages), but as observers such as Davies and Law have argued,[33] and indeed, Carew proves, this was not always the case. Roscarrock and Carew, then, provide useful insights into the emergent philosophy of Cornwall, but it is to a later period we must cast our gaze in order to see just where the paradox in Cornish philosophy really begins to open up.

---

33 C. Davies and J.E. Law (eds.), *The Renaissance and the Celtic Countries*, (Oxford, 2005).

3

The Enlightenment
versus Romanticism
Steam Engines vie with Cromlechs

Whilst the Renaissance ushered in a wave of new thought across Europe and, in the late 15th century, in Cornwall itself, the next major cultural and intellectual movement was the Enlightenment. Sometimes labelled the "Age of Reason", this movement began to develop at the tail end of the Renaissance and, as Porter has shown, those who embraced this key change in thought valued reason and science, and challenged ideas rooted in tradition, faith, and superstition.[34] Knowledge would be advanced by science and engineering. The perception of Humanity's place in the world was shaken up by several new discoveries in nature and medicine. The old Christian order had not quite crumbled (that was to come later with Darwinism[35]), but it was certainly challenged—for example, in the development of Nonconformity, in which Cornwall played a significant role.[36] Arguably, Cornwall was at the forefront of these scientific and engineering developments and the main figures of Cornish technological innovation—John

---

34 R. Porter, *Enlightenment: Britain and the Creation of the Modern Mind* (London, 2000).

35 See various contributors in S. Regan (ed.), *The Nineteenth-Century Novel: A Critical Reader* (New York and London, 2001).

36 See C. Thomas and J. Mattingly, *The History of Christianity in Cornwall AD500-2000* (Truro, 2000).

Couch Adams, John Arnold, William Clift, Humphry Davy, William Gregor, Goldsworthy Gurney, Henry Trengrouse, and Richard Trevithick—were heavily involved.[37] In general, as Rowe espouses, Cornwall was to have a front-row place in the industrial revolution[38] and this mind-set clearly defined Cornish philosophy during this period, although there has not been much written about it. An exception could be Francis Trevithick's *Life of Richard Trevithick*, which, as well as exploring the technological innovation of his father, looks also at the reasoning and logic behind his decisions.[39]

The Age of Enlightenment ran from around 1650 to 1800, though its latent effect was noticeable in Cornwall for much of the nineteenth century. Around 1800 came a new movement to counter the Enlightenment's focus on reason and place a new emphasis on emotion, feeling, nature, and place. This was Romanticism.[40] Reacting against the scientific rationalization of nature, the Romantics expressed themselves most forecefully in the arts. The Romantic period also saw the emergence what we may term of "Celticism" and a renewed interest in the cultural identity and ethnicity of the constituent parts of the Atlantic archipelago. Certainly, as Carruthers and Rawes have noted, the gaze of English Romantics was constantly drawn to the culture, thought, and landscapes of the Celtic periphery.[41] In this monograph we are particularly interested in the Cornish experience of the disparity between the two competing strands

---

37 See various entries in M. Smelt, *101 Cornish Lives* (Penzance, 2006).

38 J. Rowe, *Cornwall in the Age of the Industrial Revolution* (St Austell, 1993 [1953]).

38 F. Trevithick, *Life of Richard Trevithick: With an Account of His Inventions, Vols 1 and 2* (Cambridge, 2011 [1872]).

40 For an overview, see S. Bygraves (ed.), *Romantic Writings* (Milton Keynes and London, 1996).

41 G. Carruthers and A. Rawes (eds.), *English Romanticism and the Celtic World* (Cambridge, 2003).

of technological Enlightenment and Celtic Romanticism.[42] This philosophical phenomenon may as much define an indigenous worldview in contemporary Cornwall as the gap between "Celtic nation" and "English country".

Two Anglo-Cornish poets emphasize this shift in the Cornish worldview. One of these was Charles Valentine Le Grice (1778–1858). Generally neglected,[43] Le Grice was, in fact, part of William Wordsworth and Samuel Taylor Coleridge's "romantic" literary group. Born in Norfolk, Le Grice moved to Trereife House, near Newlyn, in effect marginalizing himself from the English literary and philosophical mainstream. In his poetry he eloquently depicted an ancient Cornwall in decay and reflected upon it as the Age of Enlightenment came to a close.[44] This is most evident in the highly philosophical poem "Inscription for Lanyon Cromlech in its Fallen State" (1823):

> And Thou at last art fall'n: Thou, who hast seen
> The storms and calms of twice ten hundred years.
> The naked Briton here has paused to gaze
> Upon thy pond'rous mass, ere bells were chimed,
> Or the throng'd hamlet smok'd with social fires.
> Whilst thou hast here respos'd, what numerous tribes,
> That breath'd the breath of life, have pass'd away.—
> What wond'rous changes in th'affairs of men!
> Their proudest cities lowly ruins made;
> Battles, and sieges, empires lost and won;
> While thou hast stood upon the silent hill

---

42 For some useful observations on this, see B. Deacon, "'The hollow jarring of the distant steam engines': images of Cornwall between West Barbary and the Delectable Duchy" in E. Westland (ed.), *Cornwall: The Cultural Construction of Place* (Newmill, 1997), pp. 7-24.

43   See. for example, W. R. Owens and H. Johnson (eds.), *Romantic Writings: An Anthology* (Milton Keynes, 1998).

44 A. M. Kent (ed.), *Charles Valentine Le Grice: Cornwall's 'Lost' Romantic Poet—Selected Poems* (St Austell, 2009).

A lonely monument of time that were. –
Lie, where thou art. Let no rude hand remove,
Or spoil thee; for the spot is consecrate
To thee, and Thou to it: and as the heart
Aching with thoughts of human littleness
Asks, without hope of knowing, whose the strength
That poised thee here; so ages yet unborn
(O! humbling, humbling thought!) may vainly seek,
What were the race of men, that saw thee fall.[45]

This concern with "lament", "loss", and "decay" is a potential marker of Cornish philosophy and something we shall explore further in this monograph. Much has been lost throughout Cornish history so this is a valid direction of enquiry. It is an elegiac paradigm even found in the motto of the Federation of Old Cornwall Societies (founded 1924): "*Kyntelleugh an brewyon es gesys na vo kellys travyth*" 'Gather ye the fragments that are left, that nothing be lost'.[46] Le Grice, however, could not fully embrace the two polarities present. Instead, it was John Harris (1820-84),[47] who managed to synthesize the two; fervently blending in his work the technological successes of mining and the Romantic view of nature, as in this excerpt from "Christian Heroism":

Hast ever seen a mine? Hast ever been
Down in its fabled grottoes, walled with gems,
And canopied with torrid mineral belts,
That blaze within the fiery orifice?
Hast ever, by the glimmer of the lamp,
Or the fast-waning taper, gone down, down,

---

45   Ibid., p.53.
46   See http://www.oldcornwall.org. Accessed 13 April 2013.
47   See P. Newman, *The Life and Poetry of John Harris (1820-84)* (Redruth, 1994).

Towards the earth's dread centre, where wise men
Have told us that the earthquake is conceived,
And great Vesuvius hath his lava-house,
Which burns and burns for ever, shooting forth
As from a fountain of eternal fire?
Hast ever heard, within this prison-house,
The startling hoof of Fear? the eternal flow
Of some dread meaning whispering to thy soul?[48]

In such poetry, Harris embraces these twin threads of Cornish philosophical experience, making him an important poet for Cornwall and, perhaps, Britain as a whole. It certainly explains why his work has been re-evaluated over the past half a century and is now considered profoundly relevant to the Cornish experience and worldview.[49] As we shall later see, however, he was also not averse to extolling the virtues of druids and cromlechs.

There have, of course, been further developments in wider philosophical thought in the twentieth and twenty-first centuries. Structuralism and Post-Structuralism have informed the work of scholars across academia,[50] and have likewise come to inform Cornish Studies and Celtic Studies. In addition, there have been useful developments in Cultural Nationalism and Ethno-symbolism.[51] Issues involving the philosophy of language have become important, as have debates surrounding

---

48 A. M. Kent (ed.), *Voices from West Barbary: An Anthology of Anglo-Cornish Poetry 1549-1925* (London, 2000), p.125.

49 See D. M. Thomas (ed.) *Songs from the Earth: Selected Poems of John Harris, Cornish Miner, 1820-84* (Padstow, 1977); A.M. Kent, *The Literature of Cornwall: Continuity, Identity, Difference 1000-2000* (Bristol, 2000), pp.113-9.

50. See relevant sections in K. M. Newton (ed.), *Twentieth-Century Literary Theory* (Basingstoke, 1988), pp. 131-70);

51 A. S. Leoussi and S. Grosby (eds.), *Nationalism and Ethno-symbolism: History. Culture and Ethnicity in the Foundation of Nations* (Edinburgh, 2007).

the protection of minority languages and the place and position of dialect.[52] No survey of philosophical trends of recent years can be fully comprehensive, given the length of this monograph. The above is intended only as a series of pointers for those researchers working in the field of Cornish Studies. In the next chapter I will begin to demonstrate in more detail the connections between philosophy and Cornwall.

---

52 D. Nettle and S. Romaine, *Vanishing Voices: The extinction of the world's languages* (Oxford, 2000); S. S. Mufwene, *The Ecology of Language Evolution* (Cambridge, 2001); R. Penhallurick (ed.), *Debating Dialect: Essays on the Philosophy of Dialect Study* (Cardiff, 2000).

4

Philosophical Visitors to Cornwall

The links between Cornwall and the modern field of philosophy are well-attested. Visiting philosophers have often used Cornwall as a "well-spring" of energy for their thinking. During the early 1920s, the British philosopher, historian, and social critic Bertrand Russell (1872–1970) and his second wife Dora Russell (1894–1986) bought the house named Carn Voel (Cornish: probably 'axe outcrop'), just above Porthcurno in West Cornwall, in order to write and bring up their children.[53] Russell was born in Monmouthshire into one of the most prominent aristocratic families in Britain, but this did not stop him becoming the leader of the British "revolt against idealism" in the early half of the twentieth century.[54] A champion of anti-imperialism and an anti-war activist (he was sent to prison for his views during the First World War[55]), Russell later championed humanitarian ideals and freedom of thought. Many of the texts he wrote during the first half of the twentieth-century were conceived while he was living and working at Carn Voel.

Dora Russell (née Black), like her husband, also engaged in politics and radical social reform. Dora Black had met Russell

53 A. Wood, *Bertrand Russell: The Passionate Sceptic* (London:, 1957); K. Tait, *My Father Bertrand Russell* (London, 1977).
54 P. A. Schilipp (ed.), *The Philosophy of Bertrand Russell* (Evanston and Chicago, 1944); A. J. Ayer, *Russell* (London, 1972).
55 Cf. S. Dalley, "The Response to the Outbreak of the First World War" in P. Payton (ed.), *Cornish Studies: Eleven* (Exeter, 2003), pp.85-109.

while on a walking tour in 1916 and supported him during his campaign against military conscription.[56] Initially, she resisted marriage to him because like many other radical women of her day, she realized that the laws of marriage were biased in favour of men.[57] As an activist she campaigned for better information about birth control,[58] and later became a famous advocate of the peace movement, joining the Campaign for Nuclear Disarmament with other left-wing thinkers of the period (among them J.B. Priestly and Michael Foot). Dora Russell also spent time at Carn Voel writing and thinking, and her life there has been documented by her daughter Katharine Tait.[59]

During the twentieth century this far south-western part of Cornwall was a magnet for a number of radical thinkers, philosophers, and writers. A stone's throw from Carn Voel, Rowena Cade developed the overtly anti-Metropolitan and Neo-Celtic Minack Theatre during the 1930s,[60] and on the north coast, Zennor witnessed the arrival of D. H. Lawrence (1885–1930).[61] A little further east along the south coast could be found the radical artistic colony at Lamorna,[62] once the temporary home of the surrealist artist and esoteric philosopher Ithell Colquhoun (1906–1988), who later came to live permanently at Paul.[63] According to some sources, Lamorna

56. D. Spender (ed.), *The Dora Russell Reader: 57 Years of Writing and Journalism* (London, 1977).

57. D. Russell, *Hypatia. Women and Knowledge* (London, 1925).

58 D. Russell, *In Defence of Children* (London, 1933).

59 K. Tait, *Carn Voel: My Mother's House* (Newmill, 1998).

60 A. M. Kent, *The Theatre of Cornwall: Space. Place, Performance* (Bristol, 2010), pp.435-9.

61 P. Payton, *D..H, Lawrence and Cornwall* (Truro, 2009); Jane Costin, *D.H. Lawrence's Quest for Blood-Consciousness: From Cornwall to America*, Ph.D thesis (Exeter, 2011).

62. See A. Wormleighton, *A Painter Laureate: Lamorna Birch and His Circle* (Bristol, 1993).

63 See R. Shillitoe, *Ithell Colquhoun: Magician Born of Nature* (USA, 2010);

was also frequently visited by the Occult philosopher Aleister Crowley (1875–1947), who came to Cornwall to visit its stone circles and monuments, seeking spiritual affinity with his own beliefs.[64]

Bertrand and Dora Russell were clearly operating in radical circles during their lifetime. Considering their interest in anti-imperialism,[65] it is perhaps paradoxical that there was no wider engagement with the politics of the early Cornish Revival. Perhaps the Russells considered Cornwall a part of wider England during this phase, or that their philosophical interest was somehow bigger than this small revival of identity, culture, and language occurring on the periphery of Britain. Either way, in their published work or private correspondence there seems little awareness of developments under their noses at Carn Voel.[66] Cade may be assessed differently since her radical proposals for an alternative theatre space were to have a lasting effect.[67] Lawrence disliked the Cornish intensely but understood their inherent Celticity and brought them to the attention of a wider reading public in the chapter devoted to Cornwall in his 1923 work *Kangaroo*.[68] Colquhoun and Crowley may be viewed as the forerunners of an interest in the philosophy of the ancient stones and monuments of Cornwall, which came

E. Ratcliffe, *Ithell Colquhoun: Pioneer Surrealist Artist, Occultist, Writer, and Poet* (Oxford, 2007).

64. See P. Newman, *The Tregerthen Horror: Aleister Crowley, D. H. Lawrence and Peter Warlock in Cornwall* (St Austell, 2005).

65. The poet Rabindranth Tagore (1861-1941) stayed with the Russells at Carn Voel. Tagore is widely regarded as an important writer in the modern Indian Renaissance and was a critic of British Imperialism in India. See K. K. Dyson (ed. and tr.), *Rabindranth Tagore: I won't Let You Go – Selected Poems* (Tarset, 1991).

66 See Dora Russell Papers held at the Institute of Social History, Amsterdam and Bertrand Russell Archives at McMaster University. Hamilton, Ontario.

67 A. Demuth. *The Minack Open-Air Theatre* (Newton Abbot, 1968).

68. D. H. Lawrence, *Kangaroo* (Harmondsworth, 1980[1923]), pp.235-87.

to a height with the work of John Michell,[69] and over more recent years has been enhanced by observations made by scholars such as Straffon, Millar, Broadhurst, and Cope.[70]

Also operating in West Cornwall—more specifically at Porthleven—was Christopher Caudwell (1907–1937), the Marxist philosopher, writer, and poet. Caudwell was born Christopher St. John Spriggs in Putney in south-west London and later joined the Communist Party, becoming interested in Marxist philosophy and trying to apply it in daily life. Caudwell stayed at the Atlantic Inn, in Porthleven, near Helston,[71] from August to October 1935 completing the work *Illusion and Reality: A Study of the Sources of Poetry*.[72] The following year he joined the International Brigade, taking part in the Spanish Civil War and was killed in action there in 1937, with his study emerging shortly after his death. Although somewhat ignored in its time, *Illusion and Reality* was part of the origin of British Marxist literary studies which would culminate in the work of later key thinkers such as Raymond Williams, Terry Eagleton (both in particular concerned with issues of philosophy and identity in Wales and Ireland respectively), and Alan Sinfield (concerned with post-war British identity).[73] Crucially, Caudwell worked within the Marxist framework of base and superstructure and argued that both the poetic form and the

---

Cf. H. Dunmore, *Zennor in Darkness* (Harmondsworth, 1994)

69 J. Michell, *The Old Stones of Land's End* (London, 1974).

70 C. Straffon, *Pagan Cornwall: Land of the Goddess* (St Just-in-Penwith, 1993) H. Millar and P. Broadhurst, *The Sun and the Serpent: An Investigation into Earth Energies* (Launceston, 1989); J. Cope. *The Modern Antiquarian: A Pre-millennial Odyssey Through Megalithic Britain including a Gazetteer to Over 300 Prehistoric Sites* (London, 2011 [1998]).

71. A plaque commemorating his stay was placed on the Atlantic Inn in 2007. This was organized by Dr James Whetter of the Roseland Institute and Porthleven Old Cornwall Society.

72 C. Caudwell, *Illusion and Reality: A Study of the Sources of Poetry* (London, 1937).

73 See, for example. R. Williams, *Problems in Materialism and Culture: Selected*

content are determined by the economic base—a form of reasoning that predated much Cultural Materialist and New Historicist literary and philosophical enquiry. It would be wrong-headed to say that Cornwall influenced the construction of such a work (indeed, this would not be what Caudwell would have argued at all) and yet, as Whetter notes, perhaps the timing and place of its evolution as a manuscript were significant.[74] Cornwall, it seems, offered the ambitious Caudwell the right conditions for its production: he produced a work that would fly in the face of contemporary New Criticism and the philosophy of elitist commentators such as F.R. Leavis.[75] Indeed, one might go further and suggest that Caudwell's contribution in *Illusion and Reality* and in successive posthumous works,[76] eventually came to define part of the post-war crisis in both English and, later, Cultural Studies, [77]— in so doing, partly allowing a field such as Cornish Studies to develop.

Other thinkers have engaged with the cultural geography of Cornwall in order to develop their philosophy. Carl Gustav Jung (1875–1961) was not really a philosopher in the purest sense, but his ideas on psychiatry and psychology have been profoundly influential on religion, literature, and philosophy.[78]

Essays (London, 1980); R. Gable (ed.), *Raymond Williams: Resources of Hope—Culture, Democracy, Socialism* (London and New York, 1989); T. Eagleton, *The Truth About the Irish* (New York, 2001), *Heathcliff and the Great Hunger: Studies in Irish Culture* (London, 1995); A. Sinfield, *Society and Literature* (London, 1983).

74 J. Whetter, *A British Hero: Christopher St John Sprigg aka Christopher Caudwell* (Gorran, 2011).

75 See entries in Newton, op.cit., pp.39-56 and pp.65-74.

76 C. Caudwell, *Studies in A Dying Culture* (Whitefish, Montana, 2010 [1938]), *Romance and Realism: Study in English Bourgeois Literature* (Princeton, 1992 [1970]).

77 For more on this, see A. West, *Crisis and Criticism, and Literary Essays* (London, 1975).

78 C. G. Robert Aziz, *C. G. Jung's Psychology of Religion and Synchronicity*

The Swiss-born Jung developed the concept of analytical psychology over a number of years.[79] In short, this is a process of integrating opposites, including the conscious with the unconscious whilst maintaining their relative autonomy. Jung's thinking was that this balance was central in human development. In order to achieve this aim, Jung spent much of his life exploring both Western and Eastern philosophy as well as areas of the occult.[80] Jung was somewhat influenced by the writings of Sigmund Freud but later deviated from him in his understanding of the unconscious. One of Jung's acolytes was Constance Long (born in Reading in 1913) who organized a seminar led by Jung in Cornwall in 1920. Cornwall again seemed to be attractive because of its esoteric past and she and Jung went walking on the Cornish cliff paths. The seminar itself was held in Sennen Cove.[81] According to her own writings, Long had a number of dreams while she was staying at Sennen Cove following Jung's seminar sessions. On 3 October, she recorded a "phantasy" that involved a "gold ring—symbol of transcendent function".[82] The Jungian method involved the use of archetypes to help people understand his ideas in Cornwall he used Wagnerian elements to get across the main points of his new religious outlook. Although Jung's time in Cornwall was comparatively short, it seems the experience in the territory prompted further key developments in his thinking, ultimately allowing for the completion of his life's work on analytical psychology.

(New York, 1990)

79　C. G. Jung, *Analytical Psychology: Its Theory and Practice—The Tavistock Lectures* (London, 1990 [1968]).

80　For an overview, see C. G. Jung. *The Archetypes and the Collective Unconscious: Collected Works of C. G. Jung* (London and New York, 1991).

81　See "The Passion of Constance Long", chapter 11 of *The Aryan Christ: The Secret Life of Carl Jung* on http://www.american-buddha.com/lit.aryanchristjung.11.htm. Accessed on 12 April 2013.

82　Ibid.

Often spoken of in the same breath as Jung is the Austrian philosopher Rudolph Steiner (1861–1925). Although some of Steiner's theories and observations have been dismissed by modern philosophy, his influence has been enormous.[83] One of his core desires was to uncover a link between science and mysticism—which he later termed "spiritual science". This was developed in order to provide a cognitive path between Western philosophy and the spiritual needs of the individual human being. This was later developed into forms of artistic exploration—in education, art, music, literature, and drama, and finally into the concept of "ethical individualism".[84] Essentially, Steiner believed that there are no limits to human knowledge. In the development of these three main phases of his work, Steiner examined a number of critical factors in Western philosophy: two of which were druidism and Arthuriana. With the druids, Steiner was interested in what Welburn later termed the "esoteric wisdom and the spirit of the Ancient Celts"[85] and in so doing, Steiner examined these ancient "mysteries" as being fundamental to understanding the human condition.

Steiner had also begun investigating the figure of King Arthur early on in his career and proposed that "King Arthur was a high initiate who made known the wisdom of the mysteries to his pupils". He posited that Arthur was an important figure for the pre-Christian mysteries and that Tintagel was a spiritual centre. Writing initially at distance from the locale, Steiner finally went there (on the westward facing cliffs of North Cornwall) on 17 August 1924 and gave a lecture on his ideas about King Arthur, the Knights of the

---

83 See G. Childs, *Rudolph Steiner: His Life and Work—An Illustrated Biography* (Edinburgh, 1995), *Steiner Education in Theory and Practice* (Edinburgh, 1991).

84 R. McDermott, *The Essential Steiner* (London, 1984).

85 A. Welburn (ed.), *The Druids: Esoteric Wisdom of the Ancient Celtic Priests— Selections from the work of Rudolf Steiner* (Forest Row, 2001).

Round Table, and Tintagel itself.[86] He also spoke about this excursion in Torquay on 21 August and in London on 27 August 1924.[87] As Thomas has noted, "Cornwall 1920–30 was the Arthurian decade par excellence",[88] so Steiner's presence is entirely fitting in a landscape that was not only developing its tourism around Arthuriana (from the 1890s onwards, the King Arthur Castle Hotel and a proposed [but ultimately abandoned] railway line to it) but also in its own esoteric symbolism (the development of a Masonic order and King Arthur's Hall in 1933).

We also note that only four years later the first modern Cornish Gorsedd was held in 1928, with its ceremonial mantra of *Nynsyu Marow Myghtern Arthur* [You are not dead King Arthur] carrying a certain mysticism that entirely fitted the perception of Steiner of such Celticity as the "esoteric wisdom" of the ancient Britons.[89] The philosophical impact of Steiner's connection to Tintagel is significant; not only in the number of New Age and Neo-Pagan shops and outlets in present-day Tintagel but also in the on-going promotion of Steiner's Arthurian philosophies. Richard Seddon's influential 1990 work. *The Mystery of King Arthur* picks up the narrative of the "Matter of Arthur" proposed by Steiner, with chapter headings such as "Battles of the Soul" and "Trials of the Spirit".[90] It would also be fair to say that recent writings by scholars such

---

86 R. Steiner, *Esoteric Lessons 1904-1909* (Forest Row, 2007), p.427.

87 Recorded by Steiner in D.S. Osmond (ed. and tr.), *Rudoph Steiner: Karmic Relationships, Vol 8* (London, 1975).

88 C. Thomas, "Hardy and Lyonesse: Parallel Mythologies" in M. Hardie (ed.), *A Mere Interlude: Some literary visitors to Lyonesse* (Newmill, 1992), pp.13-26.

89 See R. Lyon, *Gorseth Kernow / The Cornish Gorsedd: What it is and what it does* (Cornwall, 2008); Gorseth Kernow, *Ceremonies of the Gorsedd of the Bards of Cornwall* (Cornwall, n.d.).

90 R. Seddon, *The Mystery of Arthur at Tintagel* (London, 1990).

as Paul Broadhurst and Robin Heath have continued the philosophical investigation of Arthuriana.[91]

Rings (Jung) and returning kings (Steiner) had another champion connected with the western periphery of Britain. J.R.R. Tolkien (1892–1972) can also be considered to have a number of literary-philosophical links to Cornwall. Although primarily fantasy novels (establishing the genre in the modern era), a number of critics have commented on the philosophical nature of Tolkien's works such as *The Hobbit* (1937), *Lord of the Rings* (1954–5) and *The Silmarillion* (1977). Observers from several different disciplines such as Burns, Fimi, and Stephen write in various ways on the range of philosophies established in these works.[92] Tolkien himself developed a number of essays which examined the philosophical basis of his work.[93] The connection to Cornish Studies is that in the interwar years Tolkien made several visits to Cornwall and had in his own library a number of Cornish-language texts—amongst them an uncut copy of Whitley Stokes' 1872 edition of *Bewnans Meriasek, The Life of St Meriasek, Bishop and Confessor: A Cornish Drama*,[94] which we are bound to link (despite him not reading the whole text) with the naming of one of the wayward hobbits from *Lord of the Rings*—Meriadoc Brandybuck.

According to commentators such as Phelpstead, although Tolkien is most readily associated with the literature and philosophy of Anglo-Saxon, Norse, and early English culture,

---

91 P. Broadhurst and R. Heath, *The Secret Land: The Origins of Arthurian Legend and the Grail Quest* (Launceston, 2009).

92 M. Burns, *Perilous Realms: Celtic and Norse in Tolkien's Middle-Earth*, (Toronto and London, 2006); D. Fimi, *Tolkien, Race and Cultural History* (Basingstoke, 2010); E. M. Stephen, *Hobbit to Hero: The Making of Tolkien's King* (Moreton in Marsh, 2012).

93 C. Tolkien (ed.), *J.R.R. Tolkien: The Monsters and the Critics and Other Essays* (London, 2006).

94 See C. Phelpstead, *Tolkien and Wales: Language, Literature and Identity* (Cardiff, 2011), p.130. For *Bewnans Meriasek*, see W. Stokes (ed. and

there is now compelling evidence that Tolkien was highly aware of Brythonic culture in all its manifestations and that he viewed Breton and Cornish as much more representative of the original British culture than Welsh.[95] Professor Nick Groom of the University of Exeter went a stage further on 19 May 2001 when in a lecture titled "Tolkien in Cornwall" at Fowey, Cornwall he argued that there were "intimate connections between Tolkien's work and his visits to the Cornish coast", suggesting "that Cornwall may indeed be considered as the imaginative gateway to Middle-Earth".[96] We should always be sceptical of this kind of biographical criticism—relying on more accurate forms of literary criticism such as Caudwell's emergent Cultural Materialism and New Historicism—and yet, the literary-philosophical connections continue between Tolkien and Cornwall with the posthumous publication of Tolkien's *The Fall of Arthur* (2013).[97]

It is clear that all of the intellectuals above were seeking some form of philosophical enlightenment from an affinity with either Cornwall's position on the periphery or its mysterious Celticity. Both, it seems, offer philosophers from various traditions a "lightning rod" into alternative understandings of the workings of the world. In Groom's terms, Cornwall continues to be an "imaginative gateway". One only has to look at the contributions to Hale and Payton's *New Directions in Celtic Studies* (2000) or to Harvey *et al*'s 2001 collection *Celtic Geographies: Old Cultures. New Times*.[98] A more recent contribution to this understanding of the philosophy behind the

tr.), *The Life of St Meriasek, Bishop and Confessor: A Cornish Drama* (London and Berlin, 1872).

95 Ibid., pp. 89-104.

96 N. Groom, "Tolkien in Cornwall" in *The Daphne du Maurier Festival of Arts and Literature, Fowey, Cornwall Programme 2010* (Fowey, 2010), p.23.

97 Christopher Tolkien (ed.), *J.R.R. Tolkien: The Fall of Arthur* (London, 2013).

98 A. Hale and P. Payton (eds.), *New Directions in Celtic Studies* (Exeter,

Celtic experience has been the volume on *Mysticism. Myth and Celtic Identity* edited by Gibson, Trower, and Tregidga.[99]

The key issue here is that there is a paradox between those seeking philosophy in the land of the "Celtic" West Britons and the West Britons whose philosophy seems to have been neglected or dismissed; thus Cornwall inspires philosophy but has not generated its own. As we have seen, Cornwall is often presented in culture and literature as being "inspirational" and a vehicle for the "imaginative gateway" of those from outside the community and territory seeking "truth". But what of the philosophy of those on the inside? Ironically, what is "inspirational" to the visitor is often representative of hardship and austerity to the indigenous population. Given the obsession with Celticity and its apparent relationship to the field of philosophy we might expect a forceful link to be asserted, yet as we shall now consider, the paradigm between what may be perceived as "Celtic" and "Non-Celtic" in Cornwall is also deeply flawed.

2000); D. C. Harvey, R. Jones, N. McInroy and C. Milligan (eds.), *Celtic Geographies: Old Culture. New Times* (London and New York, 2002).

99 M. Gibson, S. Trower and G. Tregidga (eds.), *Mysticism. Myth and Celtic Identity* (Abingdon and New York, 2013). This collection of essays represents papers given at the "Mysticism, Myth. Nationalism" conference held at the University of Exeter's Tremough campus in July 2010.

5

From Identity Theory to Philosophy

After Ivey

In the modern era, some of the initial work completed on a native Cornish philosophy was done by the Massachusetts-based scholar Allen E. Ivey. In the period 1993–95, Ivey began investigating issues of identity theory with the Cornish in mind. Although trained as psychologist and psychiatrist, Ivey's work on Cornwall did at least begin to address some of the issues related to the formation of a native Cornish philosophy. Ivey had spent a number of years working on minority communities (including Native Americans) elsewhere and used techniques of "micro-counselling" and "media therapy" to engender renewed senses of identity amongst either oppressed or marginalized peoples.[100] This work was completed in seminar sessions and via questionnaires to open up debate about core issues of belonging, continuity, community, and ownership—related to history, language, and education in particular. He

---

100 S. G. Weinrach, "Micro-counselling and Beyond: A Dialogue with Allen Ivey" in *Journal of Counselling and Development*, Vol. 65, No.10, (1987), pp. 332-7.; A. E. Ivey, "Psychotherapy as Liberation: Towards Specific Skill and Strategies in Multicultural Counselling and Therapy" (Unpublished paper, 1994); "Media Therapy: Educational Change Planning for Psychiatric Patients" in *Journal of Counselling Psychology*, Vol. 20, No.4 (1973) pp. 336-43.

had been much influenced by other practitioners in the field of dealing with oppressed groups across the world.[101]

Part of Ivey's paradigm was that psychotherapy for the Cornish as both individuals and community could lead to what he would term "liberation", since it would stop the individual and group from being "repressed". Such liberation from repression had been seen emerging in a number of organizations and individuals, who had considered such an approach in fields as varied as politics, and economics,[102] theatre, and literature.[103] Very often such a voice came from a shared sense of oppression with other small nations or territories in the European or global community.[104] Looking back on this period, we can now also see the cultural, political, and economic movements which have helped to further shift the move to "liberation" in the Cornish mind.[105] The huge shifts towards devolution and the "break up" of Britain from 1997

101 See, for example. A. O. Ogbonnaya, "Person as Community: An African Understanding of the Person as Intrapsychic Community" in *Journal of Black Psychology*, February (1994), pp. 75-87; David Van Biema, "Who is Indian?" in *Time*. 31 October (1994), pp.73-4.

102 B. Deacon. A. George and R. Perry, *Cornwall at the Crossroads: Living Communities or Leisure Zone?* (Redruth, 1988); R. Perry, "Economic Change and 'Opposition' Policies" in Payton (ed), op.cit. (1993), pp.48-83.

103 A. M. Kent, *Out of the Ordinalia* (St Austell, 1995); Kent, op.cit. (2000), pp. 699-841.

104 M. Keating, *State and Regional Nationalisms: Territorial Politics and the European State* (London, 1988); S. Macdonald (ed.), *Inside European Identities: Ethnography in Western Europe* (Oxford and Providence. RI, 1993); P. Lynch, *Minority Nationalism and European Integration*, (Cardiff, 1996).

105 S. Parker (ed.), *Cornwall Marches On! / Keskerdh Kernow* (Truro, 1998); R.A. Pascoe (ed.), *Cornwall: One of the Four Nations of Britain* (Redruth, 1996); J. Angarrack, *Breaking the Chains: Propaganda, Censorship, Deception and the Manipulation of Public Opinion in Cornwall* (Camborne, 1999); A. M. Kent, *Celtic Cornwall: Nation, Tradition, Invention* (Wellington, 2012); B. Deacon, *The land's end: the great sale of Cornwall* (Redruth, 2013).

FROM IDENTITY THEORY TO PHILOSOPHY

onwards, have also focused some aspects of the Cornish mind on opportunities for more devolved power.[106]

Ivey's practice was to initially target gatherings of Cornish individuals and to encourage them to take part in seminar discussion groups, to talk openly about the repression felt, and to complete his questionnaires. Although in theory a useful mechanism of research, inevitably the research conducted was completed in scenarios where the individuals concerned already had a sense of oppression and liberation (for example, at Cornwall's premier Celtic festival, *Lowender Peran*), and were therefore sharply attuned to the counselling sessions offered. Therefore the "philosophy" emerging was somewhat biased in its findings. However, it has to be said that those findings were still interesting because they categorized and expressed what the Cornish felt about themselves.

Ivey's major research tool was his *Kernow Kynsa! Reclaming Your Cornish Identity* questionnaire.[107] In this document recipients were asked multiple-choice questions based on a number of historical propositions. Among these were the rejection of writing by the druidic and Celtic traditions, the Celtic Catholic church, King Arthur, the concept of "England", Glasney College, the Reformation, the Norman Conquest, the 1497 rebellion, the Crown and the Gentry, the Spanish Armada, steam technology, emigration, the Industrial Revolution, the lack of a university, and the English. These were chosen because they represented, for Ivey, core moments in the development of the Cornish psyche, and touchstones indicating how Cornish philosophy might have evolved.

---

106   Dix, op.cit.; A. Aughey, *Nationalism,. Devolution and the Challenge to the United Kingdom State* (London, 2001); B. Deacon, D. Cole and G. Tregidga, *Mebyon Kernow and Cornish Nationalism* (Cardiff, 2003).

107   A. E. Ivey, *Kernow Kynsa! Reclaiming Your Cornish Identity* questionnaire, n.d.. Ivey also circulated a short-lived newsletter on a similar theme, titled *Skolurion Kernow*.

Although useful in some ways, the chosen touchstones for this research were already established icons of national pride or even Cornish nationalism, and, given the already interested audience, reception of the process of enquiry was relatively easy. In some respects, to truly identify a background psychology or philosophy, Ivey perhaps needed a control where the Cornish were asked about less explicitly or overtly nationalist issues, since obviously being of nationalist persuasion is not a fundamental indicator of Cornishness. Indeed, for much of the modern era, the exact reverse may be true, and hence the difficulty of political breakthrough for parties such as Mebyon Kernow.[108]

The next tool which Ivey used in his work was a table identifying the worldviews—or, perhaps, the philosophy—of two groups.[109] These were labelled by Ivey as either "Cornish/Celtic" or "Anglo-centric" but might usefully be interpreted as Celtic and Non-Celtic. Ivey's strategy here was to establish to what extent the Cornish individual and group fitted the "Cornish/Celtic" philosophy. For this category, Ivey listed the following: "One and All, qualitative tradition, observer in relation to environment, oral tradition, equality, extended family, home sharing, 'being' view of time, matrilineal, work as a way of life, family may be the work unit, living with the land as part of the land, 'dour. difficult, permeated with romanticism, superstitious', fatalistic. 'independent, non-hierarchical', survival orientation ('making do'), feelings of inferiority, circularity of thought, intellectuals are suspect, unlikely to show emotion, and emotion accepted".[110]

The Non-Celtic or Anglo-centric philosophy was argued as being "an 'I' emphasis, positivist tradition, observer outside and controls environment, written tradition, hierarchy, nuclear

108 Deacon, Cole and Tregidga, op.cit.
109 A. E. Ivey. *Celtic/Cornish and Anglo-centric Worldviews*, n.d.
110 Ibid.

family, separateness, patriarchy, work as personal identity, individual as work unit, domination over the environment, 'sensible, practical, concerned with reality, and hierarchy', 'doing, action view of time', independent hierarchical, achievement orientation, feelings of superiority, causal linear thought, intellectuals are superior, unlikely to show emotion and emotion denied and hidden".[111] When looking at this list of characteristics, it is necessary to point out that it serves not only Non-Celtic or Anglo-centric philosophy and could be applied to a number of different peoples. However, Ivey's choices indicate that he wanted to provide a particular reading of both groups.

Conveniently, we can see that the Celtic philosophy neatly fits into a worldview that many of the philosophical visitors to Cornwall were actively seeking, and that the Non-Celtic view fits into everything they were trying to escape from. It may also be noted that the "imaginative gateway" later identified by Groom is easier to find in the former category than the latter. Likewise, the former seems very positive compared to the latter. Perhaps we should not be surprised by that. Initially, perhaps respondents to this philosophical imagining of what it meant to be Cornish may well have gone along with the qualities expressed within Ivey's reasoning. However, can a Cornish-Celtic philosophy be that simple? The answer has to be a firm no.

"One and All" might be an ideologically comfortable notion to live by but Cornish public life has often been fractured by disagreements as part of what I have termed elsewhere "peninsularity"[112]—a worldview which sees the Cornish often less jealous or annoyed with a distant neighbour or even oppressor, and more annoyed with those closer to them. The fracture is seen in the nineteenth century in the way that the

---

111   Ibid.
112   Kent. op.cit., (2010), p. 58.

dominant Christian belief system of the Cornish—Methodism—fractured into at least three groups: Wesleyan, United, and Primitive.[113] These factions eventually reunited in 1932 but the split had a lasting cultural and philosophical impact. Likewise, the revival of the Cornish language has also split into at least three different spelling systems and ideologies—among these Kernewek Kemmyn, Unified Cornish Reformed, and Modern/Late.[114] Although this split has begun to retreat (in the light of greater public recognition and European funding[115]), and we might even celebrate the fact that the Cornish language is strong enough to produce three alternative "dialects", the community knows and understands the philosophical departure points for the language's use and development. Thus "I" emphasis might be more appropriate.

Ivey's binary system presents "Celtic" in a particular way. As we know, Celtic Studies and academia in general have not always considered Cornwall to be fully Celtic; in other words, ticking the same kinds of boxes as established Celtic countries like Ireland and Wales.[116] In this sense, defining Cornish philosophy takes us back to a debate about the place and purpose of Celtic Studies, and who may and may not be defined as being in the Celtic club.[117] Ivey's model here does not quite fit Cornwall. We only have to look at three strands of the hypothesis. He observes that the Cornish have an oral tradition as opposed to a written one. Whilst it is true that the

---

113 T. Shaw, *A History of Cornish Methodism* (Truro, 1967). J.C.C. Probert, *A Sociology of Cornish Methodism* (Cornwall, 1971).

114 Dunbar and George, op.cit.; N. Williams. *Cornish Today: An Examination of the Revived Language* (Westport, 2006); R. Gendall, *Tavas a Ragadazow / The Language of My Forefathers* (Menheniot, 2000).

115 See http://www.magakernow.org.uk. Accessed 7 April 2013. This is the website of the Cornish Language Partnership.

116 A debate considered at length by Kent, op.cit. (2000), pp,25-51.

117 Henry Jenner finally gained entrance for Cornwall into the Celtic

Cornish certainly have a highly developed oral narrative heritage (eventually recorded in the works of William Bottrell, Robert Hunt, and others[118]); it also has a literary tradition that is neither fully literary in the sense of texts from, say, Ireland or Wales, but neither is it fully oral. Its predominant, surviving literary tradition from the medieval period onwards has been verse drama—effectively a combination of the two.[119]

Living with the land as part of the land seems irrevocably Celtic (the kind of union proposed by observers such as Colquhoun and even Lawrence) but the Cornish have hardly been ideal custodians. Indeed, the land has served a very distinctive purpose over a long period of time: mining and the extractive industries.[120] We know that this is an ancient activity[121] and that, over the centuries, Cornwall has showed domination over its environment: tin and copper hard rock mining, slate quarrying, and china clay excavation, to name but a few. Emigration to territories such as North, Central, and South America, Southern Africa, India, Australia, and New

Congress in 1904. See D. R. Williams (ed.). *Henry and Katharine Jenner: A Celebration of Cornwall's Culture, Language and Identity* (London, 2004).

118 W. Bottrell (ed.), *Traditions and Hearthside Stories of West Cornwall: First Series* (Penzance, 1870), (ed.), *Traditions and Hearthside Stories of West Cornwall: Second Series* (Penzance,1873), (ed.), *Traditions and Hearthside Stories of West Cornwall: Third Series* (Penzance, 1880); R. Hunt (ed.), *Popular Romances of the West of England: The Drolls:Traditions, and Superstitions of Old Cornwall (First Series)* (London, 1865), (ed.), *Popular Romances of the West of England: The Drolls: Traditions, and Superstitions of Old Cornwall (Second Series)* (London, 1865); M. A. Courtney (ed.), *Cornish Feasts and Folklore* (Exeter 1989 [1890]); A. M. Kent and G, McKinney (eds.), *The Busy Earth: A Reader in Global Cornish Literature 1700-2000* (St Austell, 2008).

119 Kent, op.cit. (2000).

120 See A. K. Hamilton Jenkin, The *Cornish Miner: An Account of his Life Above and Underground from Early Times* (Newton Abbot, 1972 [1927]); Rowe, op.cit..

121 R. Penhallurick, *Tin in Antiquity* (London,1986).

Zealand have shown that the Cornish have engendered a similar dominance on an international scale.[122] Transnationality has had little effect in moderating this. It is worth noting, then, that while mining can be "in tune" with the land, it is hardly ever environmentally friendly.

The notion of the Cornish being "dour and difficult, permeated by romanticism, [and] superstitious" may, on the other hand, be an important thread in the Cornish philosophy on life. The Cornish, to both insiders and outsiders alike, can be "dour and difficult" but this might given a more positive gloss if we consider them as sticking to their beliefs and worldview.[123] Arguably, Cornwall has been permeated with romanticism in all its manifestations throughout the ages and this romanticism is still present today. The Cornish are certainly superstitious (one only has to look at the folkloric record). However, such a view would not be entirely accurate as the Cornish are also "sensible, practical, concerned with reality and hierarchy". One may argue that the dominance of the Cornish in the field of mining and the extractive industries, as well as in fishing and agriculture, has been a result of these characteristics. Practicality has always been a by-word of the key developments in engineering and invention,[124] whilst hierarchy has dominated mining environments both at home and overseas.[125] The Cornish are usually controllers of their environments rather than observers.

Although Ivey's list needs to be qualified and carefully deconstructed, there are some aspects of his vision of Cornish

---

122 P. Payton, *The Cornish Overseas* (Fowey: 1999); Kent and McKinney, op.cit.

123 See the views of R. L. Stevenson on Cornish Miners in America in Kent and McKinney, ibid., p.100.

124 See the numerous entries on engineers and inventors in M. Smelt, *101 Cornish Lives* (Penzance, 2006).

125 Mining was always hierarchical. For the Cornish at home, see Hamilton Jenkin, op.cit. For numerous examples of fighting between

philosophy which do seem to carry a certain kind of truth. Work as a way of life seems particularly apt, as does a fatalistic view of experience (born out further in Cornu-English concepts below). It is true that for long periods of Cornish history, families were extended vehicles for employment and opportunity (hence the term "Cousin Jack" and the notion that all Cornish people are cousins).[126] Populist accounts tend to show the Cornish (and Cornishmen in particular) as unlikely to show emotion and suffer feelings of inferiority (especially seen in many theatrical and literary narratives from the seventeenth century onwards of the Cornish faced with the sophistication of London).[127]

Ivey's work was later qualified and moderated by Payton's more accurate understanding of the situation on the ground in Cornwall.[128] Although Ivey's work certainly had flaws in terms of its understanding of the Celtic/Non-Celtic axis in Cornwall as well as the group he was completing the research with, his foray into developing an initial understanding of Cornish philosophy must be praised. Since the completion of his research, although analysis of identity has continued and developed,[129] it is something of a disappointment that philosophical enquiry has not been attempted on the same scale. However, it must be mentioned that since the late 1990s, confidence in Cornwall's identity and perhaps even philosophy has increased a good deal. Popularly, to coin Ivey's phrase, this "liberation" has come about in all kinds of ways: through food

---

Irish labour and Cornish management in the USA, see A.M. Kent, *Cousin Jack's Mouth-organ: Travels in Cornish America* (St Austell, 2004).

126 See Halliday, op. cit.; Payton, op.cit.; Deacon, Schwartz and Holman, op.cit.

127 Kent, op.cit. (2000), pp. 104-46, op.cit. (2010).

128 A. E. Ivey and P. Payton, "Toward a Cornish Identity Theory" in P. Payton (ed.), *Cornish Studies: Two* (Exeter, 1994), pp.151-63.

129 See Willett, op.cit.; Dickinson, op.cit.; Dunmore, op.cit..

and drink, music, theatre, and literature.[130] The food and drink angle has embodied much of what is perceived to be good about Cornwall (almost matching Ivey's Cornish qualities); to the extent that Cornwall suddenly finds itself a food capital of Britain. The use of iconography, packaging, labelling, and product names has helped to reinforce a distinctive Cornish philosophy. Media personalities such as Rick Stein (in spite of being seen as changing the face of a traditional fishing community such as Padstow) have, along the way, also managed (for good or bad) to change perceptions of Cornishness.

It is worth noting that the conclusions Ivey came to have broadly matched later observations: that the Cornish—although Celtic—do not necessarily carry the full characteristics of the Celtic group as a whole. Some commentators have explained this paradox by positing the Cornish as "industrial Celts"—a tautology, perhaps, but one which seems to embody Cornish philosophy.[131] The website *Ty – Gwyr – Gwyryn*,[132] run by the Cornish activist Jim Pengelly, also explores what he terms the "Cornish paradox" where the Cornish recognize that they are forced to operate within an "alien system imposed on them from outside" but "seem

130 See, for example, C. Trewin and A. Woolfitt, *Gourmet Cornwall* (Penzance, 2005), *Cornish Fishing and Seafood* (Penzance, 2006); J. Howlett, "Putting the Kitsch into Kernow" in P. Payton (ed.), *Cornish Studies: Twelve* (Exeter, 2004), pp.30-60; A.M. Kent, "Alex Parks, Punks and Pipers: Toward a History of Popular Music in Cornwall 1967-2007" in P. Philip (ed.), *Cornish Studies: Fifteen* (Exeter, 2007), pp. 209-47, op.cit., (2000), pp, 699-841; P. Hayward, "Jynwethek Ylow Kernewek: The Significance of Cornish Techno Music" in P. Payton (ed.), *Cornish Studies: Seventeen* (Exeter, 2009), pp.173-87.
131 Kent, op.cit., (2000), p. 124 and p.280; P. Payton, "Industrial Celts? Cornish History in the Age of Technological Prowess" in P. Payton (ed.), *Cornish Studies: Ten* (Exeter, 2002), pp. 116-35.
132 See http://www.kernowtgg.co.uk. Accessed 8 April 2013. These three words mean 'Land, Truth, People'.

incapable of being efficient, or effective, in [their] fight against it".[133] Ivey was, of course, trying to find the tools in terms of psychological and philosophical enquiry in order to make that "liberation" both efficient and effective. In the introduction to his concise history of Cornwall,[134] the economic historian Deacon, draws on a 2002 article of mine which argued that a core issue in Cornwall is its "unresolved duality of place" and that Cornish philosophy involves people having to "work through" Cornwall's competing traditions—English county and Celtic Nation—in order to understand themselves; therefore seeking, in philosophical terms, the truth, values, and knowledge of both.[135] I also labelled this process the "cultural negotiations" which needed to take place but we may go one stage further here and argue that a more intense scrutiny is actually required. We may now be at a point where the "cultural negotiations" (embodied in the popular culture below) are clearer and that higher order, philosophical negotiations must take place. These negotiations must take place not only with those seen traditionally as the oppressors (the English nation-state, central government, the Duchy, and heritage organizations[136]) but also, more importantly amongst ourselves. This is because to identify a single Cornish philosophy at the moment is not possible because there is such a plurality of identities that pre-exist.

That said, in this world, Cornishness (in all of its manifestations) is rarely defined along philosophical lines. Crucially, unless the Cornish are prepared to make this jump to a new level of awareness of direction, purpose, and place in the global community, they will continue to be perceived as

---

133 Conversation with the author, 8 April 2013.
134 Deacon, op. cit. (2007), p.2.
135 A. M. Kent, "'In Some State...': a decade of literature and literary studies of Cornwall" in Payton, op.cit. (2002), pp. 212-39.
136 Clearly expressed in Angarrack, op.cit.

they have been in the past as a kind of moaning and lamenting periphery. Our purpose, therefore, has to be both to deconstruct Ivey's work and the work of others who have written on identity theory, and to develop those important paradigms into a more secure understanding of the range of worldviews and the history of ideas that make up a wider Cornish philosophy. This is the way in which we can reach the kind of understanding attempted by other philosophers and thinkers.[137] It is to this history of ideas we must turn next.

---

137 See, foe example, B. Anderson, *Imagined Communities: Reflections on the Origin and Spread of Nationalism* (London and New York 2006 [1983]); E/ W. Said, *Culture and Imperialism* (London, 1994), *The Question of Palestine* (New York, 2003); Noam Chomsky, *On Language* (New York, 1998), *Hopes and Prospects* (London, 2011).

6

Cornish Philosophical Origins
Glosses, Vocabulary, and Prophecy

Ironically, it is to early manuscript sources we must go to begin
to understand any possible connections and historical
continuum of native and active Cornish philosophy. The first
text that engages with philosophy is an annotation on a ninth-
century manuscript of *De Consolatione Philosophiae* [*The Consolation
of Philosophy*] of Boethius, a text primarily associated with the
circle of King Alfred. The annotation *ud rocashaas* (probably
translated to 'The mind hated the gloomy places') appears to
be Cornish and was written in a different hand than other
Latin and Old English comments.[138]

Anicius Manlius Severinus, better known as Boethius (c.475-
524) was born to a Roman consular family and studied
philosophy, mathematics, and poetry. A bold court minister
and writer, he was stripped of his titles and wealth and
executed for treason. His *The Consolation of Philosophy* argues
that everything is insecure aside from virtue. The text became
enormously influential in the Middle Ages. The Cornish
connection with this text was discovered in 2006, following
work by Malcolm Godden, Rohini Jayatilaka, and Patrick
Sims-Williams.[139] Although just a fragment of an annotation,
it does appear to show a person with knowledge of Cornish

---

138 http.admin.ox.ac.uk/po/news/2005-06/jun. Accessed 25 April
2013.

139 Ibid.

engaging with one of the wider texts of European philosophy on the issue of virtue. Not only does it indicate the inter-relationship between Alfred's court and the Cornish reader and writer, but the suggestion of thought in the note seems to show metaphorical engagement with the text being read, and therefore could indicate some small example of early native Cornish philosophy.

This thinker, though, was not the only Cornish speaker to engage with the wider early European continuum of thought. Formerly thought (before the discovery of the above fragment) to have been the earliest source of written Cornish, the nineteen glosses from Smaragdus's *Commentary on Donatus* date from around the end of the ninth century. They were originally believed to be examples of Old Breton but in 1907 Joseph Loth (1847–1934) argued that they were, in fact, Old Cornish.[140] The confusion reveals the close cultural relationship between Old Cornish and Old Breton, often so similar as to be indistinguishable. This, however, is more likely to be a Latin text that has been glossed by a Breton, but whatever the linguistic minutiae there are some striking similarities in five of the glosses to Old Cornish. These are the following: *Marchoc* [Horseman], *Fron* [Nose], *Mesin* [Acorn], *Toroc* [Tick (insect)], and *Cintil* [kinship group]. Quite why these words are glossed is unclear. However, Aelius Donatus (c.354 CE) was one of the most famous Latin grammarians of late antiquity, while Smaragdus was Exarch (Emperor) of Ravenna between the years 585–589 and 603–611. Donatus and Smaragdus thus had pan-European influence, but what is interesting in these random glosses is their focus. These are five concepts of living that are embodied in the Cornish worldview at this time. Although two are mere labels for an insect and a part of the face, the other three give more of a sense of cultural outlook

---

140 See Paris MS. Lat. 13029 (Bibliothèque Nationale). Arbois de Jubainville (1906) in *Revue Celtique*, xxvii

and value—with a focus on the kinship group and horses. Acorn meanwhile carries with it the potential for symbolism (in particular, if we take a druidic focus—of which Steiner would have approved) yet we should be sceptical. Such terms seem to suggest the Celtic type (along Ivey's lines) and whilst they appear significant, they may not be so. They may, nonetheless, be indicators of thought and the conceptualization of self during this early and predominantly oral phase.

A wider understanding of the Cornish worldview comes in a text from c.1000. This is the *Vocabularium Cornicum* [*The Old Cornish Vocabulary*]—a Cornish-Latin thesaurus probably compiled by Ælfric, the abbot of Eynsham. It classifies biblical and everyday terms for Cornish speakers learning Latin.[141] In many respects, the vocabulary is the closest we shall come to understanding the language spoken during this period and perhaps even before this period. The vocabulary is presented logically, showing the ordering of the universe. Clearly the base vocabulary shows the centrality of these objects in any philosophical understanding of the people of West Britain during this phase. The translations may again offer an insight into that native philosophy and a history of ideas during this phase.

Meanwhile, *Prophetia Merlini* [*The Prophecy of Merlin*] by John of Cornwall (c.1150) belongs to the widespread medieval tradition of expressing political and religious propaganda in the guise of ancient prophecy, drawing heavily on Cornish and Celtic mythology. Many of the references—probably political and necessarily cryptic at the time—are now obscure beyond recovery, yet its finely-crafted delirium is compelling to read and there are moments in the text which seem to draw on native philosophy, albeit in a garbled form.[142] John of

---

141   *Vocabularium Cornicum* (Cottonian or Old Cornish Vocabulary, BL MS Cotton Vespasian A XIB, London).

142   See translation offered in A. Hale, A. Kent and T, Saunders (eds.

Cornwall was probably born in St Germans in the early twelfth centuryand studied in Paris. He died sometime around 1199. Like the earlier texts, a number of glosses in Cornish on the Latin of this translation again suggest a particular worldview. The text clearly establishes a cynical view of invasion from the east, and the rise of Anglo-Saxon power—a debate which of course, has informed over one thousand years of Cornish history, and which is still important to some contemporary Cornish observers.[143]

Much of early Cornish literature has contributed to native philosophical debate. The nature and function of love, for example, is discussed in the romance of Beroul's version of *Tristan and Iseult*.[144] If we are to believe, as Jenner did, that Beroul's version of the text was probably based on that of a Cornishman or someone who knew intimately the south coast of Cornwall, then we see another strand emerging.[145] Within the expansive canon of medieval Middle Cornish drama, it is of course, a Christianized view of philosophical debate that is examined. The key biblical scenes of *Ordinalia*, as well as substantial sequences in *Bewnans Meriasek* and *Bewnans Ke*, look at considerable philosophical debates over belief in God and Jesus, and in the states of the world leading from Creation to the Resurrection (Doomsday is curiously absent).[146] These plays undoubtedly represent some of the key philosophical

and trs.), *Inside Merlin's Cave: A Cornish Arthurian Reader 1000-2000* (London, 2000), pp.42-7.

143 For a range of views, see Deacon, op.cit. (2007); Angarrack, op.cit. (2002).

144 A. S. Frederick (ed. and tr.), *Beroul: The Romance of Tristan* (London, 1970).

145 H. Jenner, "The Tristan Romance and its Cornish Provenance" in *Journal of the Royal Institution of Cornwall*, No.14 (1914), pp.464-88.

146 Several of these are discussed in Kent and Saunders, op.cit.. See also G. Thomas and N. Williams (eds. and trs.), *Bewnans Ke: The Life of St Kea—A Critical Edition with Translation* (Exeter, 2007).

debates of the Cornish during this period. Murdoch, Bakere, Thomas and Williams, and Kent have all examined the intersection of these Christianized Graeco-Roman philosophies with medieval dramaturgy.[147]

---

147 Murdoch, op.cit; J. Bakere, *The Cornish Ordinalia: A Critical Study* (Cardiff, 1980); Thomas and Williams, ibid., Kent, op.cit, (2000).

7

Philosophizing in Cornish

Richard Rufus and his Circle

Although literature gives us an insight into the relationship between Cornwall and philosophy, a more direct link is found in the figure of Richard Rufus of Cornwall, who died around 1260. Rufus' origins in Cornwall are shadowy but it is known that he was a Cornish philosopher and theologian who in the 1220s studied at Paris and Oxford.[148] In 1230 he became a Franciscan. Rufus' importance in the narrative of Cornish philosophy is due to the fact that he was one of the earliest medieval philosophers to re-engage with Aristotle and write on him. His commentaries are believed to be some of the earliest to have survived. Rufus also wrote a number of commentaries on the *Four Books of Sentences*—the standard medieval theology textbook, written by Peter Lombard (c1096–1164).[149] We know from his writings that Rufus was influenced by a number of other thinkers; among them Alexander of Hales (1185–1245). Hales is in present-day Shropshire, England, and Alexander was an important theologian of the Franciscan School.[150] Although Rufus had humble beginnings in

---

148 See "Richard Rufus of Cornwall: *In Aristotelis De Generatione et corruptione*" in R. Wood and N. Lewis, *Auctores Britannici Medii Aevi* (Oxford and New York, 2004).

149 See P. Delhaye, *Pierre Lombard: sa vie, ses œuvres, sa morale* (Paris and Montreal, 1961).

150 See C. Beiting, "The Idea of Limbo in Alexander of Hales and

Cornwall, he also became aware of the work of the founder of what may be termed the English intellectual tradition—Robert Grosseteste (c1175–1253), and Richard Fishacre (1200–1248), a Dominican, who became the first holder of the Dominican Chair at Oxford.

Opinion about Rufus as a philosopher seems to have varied greatly. Roger Bacon (c.1214–1294) believed him to be "base" in the sense that his fame was greatest with the ignorant multitude, while Thomas Eccleston (died c.1258), praised his excellence as a lecturer.[151] Another of this philosophical circle was Adam de Marisco (Adam Marsh), who was born in Bath around 1200. De Marisco knew Rufus well and, interestingly, describes him in a letter to Grossesteste as "a man lacking command of the English tongue, yet of most honest conversation and unblemished reputation, learned in human and divine literature".[152] Clearly, the reason for Rufus' lack of command of the English tongue was that he was primarily a Cornish speaker.[153] The philosophical debate between these scholars was being conducted in Latin and the fact that he was a native speaker of Cornish was no barrier to his movement around the isle of Britain or onto the European mainland.[154] Rufus is a fascinating figure to contemplate because he would clearly have been able to absorb both native Cornish philosophy of the Age with wider pan-European thought. It is also fascinating to wonder if Rufus ever returned to Cornwall to impart what key thought he had acquired in Paris and Oxford.

Bonaventure" in *Franciscan Studies*, 57 (1999), pp. 4-8.
151   Wood and Lewis. op.cit..
152   Quoted in G. G. Coulton, *Social life in Britain: from the conquest to the Reformation* (Cambridge, 1938), p.27.
153   Cf. John Trevisa. See D.C. Fowler, *The Life and Times of John Trevisa, Medieval Scholar* (Seattle and London, 1995).
154   Cf. John of Cornwall. See Hale. Kent and Saunders, op.cit.

8

"A reflex of Ancestral Experience"

One of the chief historians of medieval Cornwall, Leonard Elliott Elliot-Binns, noted the significance of Rufus in the development of Cornish philosophy.[155] Elliot-Binns' work documents the characteristics of the early Cornish people and whilst his notes almost work as an early embodiment of Ivey's identity theory, beneath the surface there are hints of a native philosophy. Far from there being a suggestion that a native philosophy is born out of one people alone, the enlightened Elliot-Binns argues that the Cornish world-view is derived from merging and coalescence with a number of other ethnic groups: Saxon, Norman, Breton (themselves returning West Britons in effect), Irish, and English.[156] He also notes the centrality of sea and seafaring in the Cornish mindset. Notions of sentimentality and place—similar to those proposed by Ivey—are also important to the Cornish, according to Elliot-Binns. He notes, for example, that with the Cornish, "there was scarcely a rock or a tree untouched by legendary sentiment" and that "almost every activity in which [the Cornishman] engaged was a kind of reflex of ancestral experience".[157] With these expressions, we perhaps move towards a neat summary of some aspect of native Cornish philosophy. Elliot-Binns goes further, however. He also notes

---

155 L. C. Elliot-Binns, *Medieval Cornwall* (London, 1953), p. 407.

156 Ibid., pp. 45-61. Cf. Kent, op.cit. (2000), pp. 22-3.

157 Ibid., p.59.

that the Cornish are "prone to be affected by the land as a whole" and are "apt to be haunted by a sense of things ancient and enchanted".[158] Here, the Cornish seem to be following Ivey's "type". This is again supported by Elliot-Binns' argument that the medieval Cornish were "apt to be emotional and imaginative, rather than logical and intellectual".[159] Again, this would seem to support Ivey's notion of Celtic—and yet Elliot-Binns tempers this assertion with the full awareness that were the Cornish not logical and intellectual, then they would not have been such masterful inventors, mariners, and migrants across the world. Here, we see the paradox of Cornish philosophy again at work.

Needless to say, Elliot-Binns also identifies a "detached and independent spirit"[160] but appears not to know if this is caused by the land's geography or the people's history—or perhaps even a combination of the two. It is important to point out that this independent spirit is evident in various manifestations of what Payton came to call "difference".[161] Yet there is internal difference and division too and Elliot-Binns perceptively notes the irony of "One and All", commenting that the Cornish are sometimes guilty of "not cooperating" with each other.[162] The scope of this monograph does not allow us to explore Elliot-Binns' observations in full but it is quite clear that as a thinker he has a clear understanding of several aspects of native philosophy. Although his work is celebrated as one of the finest studies of this period, it might be re-assessed as one of the twentieth-century's most perceptive analyses of who the Cornish are and how they think. Although imagined for the

158 Ibid., p.60.
159 Ibid., p.62.
160 Ibid., p/64.
161 P. Payton, *The Making of Modern Cornwall: Historical Experience and the Persistence of "Difference"* (Redruth, 1992).
162 Elliot-Binns. op.cit..

medieval period, many of these traits and thoughts are applicable today for the modern West Briton.

Perhaps these last vestiges of native medieval Cornish philosophy are found in the writing of William Scawen(1600-89).[163] A Vice-Warden of the Stannaries, Scawen knew intimately many parts of Cornwall and was well-placed to see "transition" occurring in both the learned and working classes. In his 1680 essay *Antiquities Cornuontanic: The Causes of Cornish Speech's Decay*, Scawen used his legalistic mind to document the reasons for the decline of Cornish. In so doing he assembled a document demonstrating the philosophy of the older, medieval Cornwall in transition to the modern, industrial Cornwall. The binary positions of what Pengelly terms the "Cornish Paradox" are found throughout his essay. Whilst Scawen effectively prefigures what Elliot-Binns later documented, between the larger passages on decline, lament and loss, and how these should be counteracted, there are insights into Cornish philosophy. Again, all these threads cannot be explored here for reasons of space, yet we note, for example, Scawen's view of the Cornish for "their want of a character" as they are lacking some kind of fighting spirit.[164] He observes that there was "a great loss of Armorica, near unto us, by friendship, by interest, by correspondence"[165] and that this loss of connection with Brittany, in some way, was harmful to the Cornish spirit, and that Cornish Philosophy would be more "complete" with an awareness of this. Scawen is interesting here, for during the twentieth century it is fair to say that there has been much re-

---

163 Matthew Spriggs, "William Scawen (1600-1689): A Neglected Cornish Patriot and Father of the Cornish Language Revival" in P. Payton (ed.), *Cornish Studies: Thirteen* (Exeter, 2005), pp. 98-125.

164 William Scawen "Antiquities Cornuontanic: The Causes of Cornish Speech's Decay" in Kent and Saunders (ed. and trs.) op.cit., pp.281-93.

165 Ibid.

engagement with Brittany; particularly on pan-Celtic, twinning, and dance lines.[166]

Also noted is what Scawen perceives as "a general stupidity [which may be] observed in the whole country".[167] Here, he becomes critical of the philosophy Carew embraced, which by 1680 had seemed to percolate not only through the landed gentry in the East, but in eight years, across the whole population of Cornwall. Cornwall's closeness to Devon is also critiqued, and Scawen seems to suggest that this dual philosophy of merger with the rest of south-West England is inevitably flawed; a debate which has resurfaced in the modern era over such issues as Tamarside, Regional Enterprise Zones, the European Union, and potential cross-border Parliamentary constituencies. One might argue that this debate over "border" (acknowledged in Carew and supported by modern experience) is fundamental in Cornish philosophy. This notion of "border" is incidentally also observed in the work of philosophers such as Raymond Williams in his understanding of the centrality of what happens when small territories meet and brush against larger ones.[168] Border humour and awareness is retained today in the Cornish mindset—in joke passports, in protest, and, as shown below, in symbol and language.

Finally we might consider what Scawen calls "the coming in of strangers".[169] This is a curious notion because it stretches far back through history to the ironic notion of Cornwall itself (Cornwall was named by the Saxons as "the horn of

---

166 See http://www.festival-interceltique.com. Accessed 25 April 2013. Several Cornish towns are twinned with ones in Brittany. The Cornish *Nos Lowen* is an adaptation of the Breton *Fest Noz*.

167 Scawen, op.cit.

168 See R. Williams, *Border Country* (London, 1960); D. L. Dworkin and L. G. Roman (eds.), *Views from the Border Country: Raymond Williams and Cultural Politics* (New York and London, 1993).

169 Scawen, op.cit.

strangers"[170]) while remaining relevant to the current debate over in-migrants, whether they are perceived as "emmets" or "interlopers", or seen as part of wider social movement across the European Union.[171] The philosophical issue is clear: given the small area of Cornwall, the "strangers" dissipate the language and culture—a wider philosophical debate for a small island such as Britain in the current economic climate. Here, Scawen appears to say that intermingling with strangers leads to the loss of the Cornish language, but the debate can easily be extended forward through the English accommodation of Cornwall to consider tourism, second-homes, and development. Such a philosophical quest from 1680, not only to preserve the Cornish language, but also seemingly an older Cornish identity is very much to the fore in Scawen's argument. His writings need further investigation not only as a last rear-guard action against Anglicization, but also as indicators of a Cornish state of mind. However, seeing as how Scawen's primary philosophical aim was the "saving" of the Cornish language, I now propose to offer some paradigms of the philosophy of two language groups in Cornwall: the Cornish language itself and that which began this monograph—Cornu-English.

170 See C. Weatherhill, *Cornish Language and Place Names* (Wilmslow, 1995), pp.1-7. Cf. N.R. Phillips, *The Horn of Strangers* (Tiverton, 1996).
171 See Payton (ed.), op.cit. (1993); Deacon, op.cit. (2013).

9

The Philosophy
of the Cornish language
Dreams, Funding, and Safety

It hardly needs saying but conducting one's life and thoughts in a language other than English gives the individual and the group a particular slant on experience. Numerous constructions, ideas, concepts, colours, animals, abstractions, and the ways of naming the world are entirely different in Cornish.[172] The structure of Cornish puts different emphasis on what is important.[173] This "difference"—embodied in a very real way in the Cornish language—is perhaps what those visiting philosophers were seeking. The Cornish language facilitates a closeness to landscape, nature, and direct experience that cannot be found in English. To truly live in another language, speakers must "dream" in Cornish—not just slip into an "I am speaking Cornish" moment to shut out non-speakers and non-Cornish, a practice which can be observed at some gatherings of Cornish speakers today. To conduct

---

172 See the numerous examples in Kent and Saunders, op.cit.. See also T. Saunders (ed.), *Nothing Broken: Recent Poetry in Cornish* (London, 2006).

173 This is articulated by a number of observers, but see P. Russell, *An Introduction to the Celtic Languages* (London and New York, 1995); Gendall, op.cit.; Piotr Stalmaszczyk, *Celtic Presence: Studies in Celtic Languages and Literatures: Irish. Scottish Gaelic and Cornish* (Łódź, 2005).

one's life in Cornish requires a philosophical decision about language, culture, and identity.

Whilst a philosophy of existence was entirely natural when Cornwall was un-anglicized, if we are honest we have to go back a very long way to find Cornwall or parts of Cornwall which were completely unaffected by other languages. Cornwall was bi-lingual comparatively early on but this has not stopped romantic visions of a "past" Cornwall being more fully Celtic and therefore extolling a more meaningful and coherent Cornu-Celtic philosophy. Like the language itself, this more fully operational Celtic world would appear to denote a kind of philosophical purity of mind about what being Cornish is, and that anything "tainted" by external influences therefore alters and corrupts the original. We are aware of this ideological construct, despite, as we have seen above in literature and philosophy, the fact that Cornwall operated on a pan-European scale and was always threading in influences from other cultures and worldviews. To this extent, this philosophic purity of Celticity is nonsensical, because it could never have existed in the first place.

One of the key social phenomena for the Cornish is the fact that some speakers of Cornish consider themselves philosophically superior to those who don't speak Cornish. Thus the non-speaker is philosophically inferior because he or she has not taken up the language. By some speakers, Cornish is seen as a hotwire into true Celticity—and that not speaking Cornish is a philosophical compromise. It is a compromise that is required on a daily basis by the media, by education, and in the workplace. The philosophical question is one that has beset the wider Cornish Revival over many years—are you any more Cornish if you are able to speak the language? Detractors would say no, because many Cornish people who have no knowledge of the language would still be able to trace their Cornishness back several generations to a time when their ancestors did speak the language. Supporters would argue that learning Cornish is the ultimate ideological commitment to distinguishing oneself from "Englishness". Likewise, a number of speakers of Cornish are not native or ethnic Cornish, but have taken the language up to have an affinity with it. This "Neo-Cornish" ideology is a particularly interesting social phenomenon, with some speakers seemingly wishing to learn the language because of its obscurity: or its Tolkienesque roots in an imaginary past. Very often, such "Neo-Cornish" study to become "Language bards" of the Cornish Gorsedd. There are many philosophical questions arising form this; not least what Neil Kennedy would term the cultural "usefulness" of this process.[174]

We may go further in our philosophical questioning of the revival of Cornish. Is it more helpful, for example, for a world-wide cinematic audience to see a few lines of Cornish with subtitles in a major feature film, or for play-goers in London to see a drama with some limited Cornish language in it? Or would it be more useful for a long, nineteenth-century novel to be translated into Cornish for learners and new speakers, or for a Cornish-language poetry booklet to be published and read amongst, say, fifty speakers? On one level, the cultural usefulness of the film or play is great because they raise awareness amongst a high number of people that a Cornish language exists. However, the impact may be temporal and not long-lasting. The novel and poetry books may not have the widespread circulation and, in effect, are consumed by a self-defined "ghetto" of speakers. Their effect amongst this small group might, nonetheless, be very great indeed. These are the questions which need to be asked about the future of Cornish.

174 Early draft of Neil Kennedy Ph.D submission to the University of Exeter: *Employing Cornish Cultures for Community Resilience.* I am grateful for Neil Kennedy allowing me access to this document.

Philosophical debate over them will inevitably sharpen the kind of culture "dreamt" of.

The Cornish Gorsedd, to an extent, believes in the philosophical model that the language of Cornish is that hotwire into Celticity. If it did not, then it would surely conduct its business in another language; most probably English. However, this philosophical purity embedded in the values of the Gorsedd could perhaps be seen as problematical. Despite in-migration, the dominant language group within Cornwall is still the Cornu-English speakers. Yet, within the ceremonies and competitions of the Gorsedd, Cornu-English has a relatively lowly position because ideologically it is not the "appropriate" language for true Celticity. That is reserved for Cornish alone—both in the ceremony and in competitions. With the latter, prizes for stories or poetry in Cornu-English are invariably light-hearted in content and never philosophically "deep".

Philosophical debate about the place and position of Cornish has underpinned much of the recent debate over the spelling and pronunciation of Revived Cornish. In general, one's point of engagement with the Cornish language is shaped according to one or another philosophical take-off point regarding the survival of the language. These need not be repeated here because the positions are well established and have been covered by a number of other observers. The complexity of this debate, however, is very important in determining point of entry, so to speak, yet in attempts to standardize the spelling and pronunciation of the different "dialects" and "systems" of the language, the Cornish Language Partnership has, in effect, had to muddy and coagulate quite distinctive philosophical waters in determining its Standard Written Form.[175]

---

175 See http://www.magakernow.org.uk. Accessed 27 April 2013. The debate over the development of the Standard Written Form may be followed in *Maga* newsletters.

One might go further and suggest that there is another paradox here. Funding for the development of Cornish from both Central United Kingdom Government and the European Union has been dependent on this philosophical muddling— something which has given concern to all sides within the contemporary Cornish-language debate. There is also a distinctive philosophical agenda to the Cornish-language Partnership which, seemingly, in its promotional literature, website, and newsletters, would have the public think that the Cornish language is much more active than it actually is.[176] The tone of its engagement with the public is that Cornish is like cabbage and is somehow "good for you". The confused agenda of the Partnership has tended to move towards populist material but it has been less keen on answering the more difficult questions within the revival of Cornish: the still relatively small number of speakers, the much needed philosophical debate, what we need the language for and what it should do, and how the language should serve the needs of native Cornish philosophy.

Another fundamental philosophical question is that of how the Cornish Language Partnership has disenfranchised many people interested in the Cornish language by being part of a bureaucratic process. The above questions are fundamental to the progress and development of the Cornish language for the twenty-first century. To conclude, whilst the Cornish Language Partnership has funded important projects such as a booklet on Cornish theatre for Schools,[177] and Will Coleman's *Tales from Porth*,[178] these two projects tend to emphasize the debate over the philosophy of Cornish language projects. The former, in particular, is "safe" and covers well-

---

176   Ibid.
177   E. Stewart, *Drama Kernewek: Cornish Medieval Drama—A Resource and Activity Pack* (Truro, 2012).
178   W. Coleman, *Tales from Porth* (Truro, 2008), *More Tales from Porth* (Truro, 2011).

trodden ground because of the close ideological association of the Celto-Catholic Mystery play culture. The same associations were being made at the start of the Revival, so in this way there is a philosophical restriction on what can and can't be done.[179] The Partnership's funding of Coleman's series is more philosophically dangerous and progressive, since it asserts an active bilingualism, and innovative artistic and sociological interaction, though it is perhaps harder to see where hoped for take-up will occur in an anglicized education system in which Cornish or Cornish History are not a distinctive part of the National Curriculum. This is truly where the philosophy of Cornish language has to engage.

---

179   See, for example. A S. D. Smith, *The Story of the Cornish Language: Its Extinction and Revival* (Camborne, 1947).

10

The Philosophy of Cornu-English

Keep Calm and Do it Dreckly

Cornu-English is likely to be a larger indicator of indigenous Cornish philosophy because, put simply, more people speak it and identify with concepts within it. As Penhallurick argues, the philosophy of all dialects of English need careful consideration.[180] Although the Cornish language might have extolled Cornish ethics and thought earlier on in history, Cornu-English is the primary means of communication for most of the indigenous population in Cornwall today.[181] Cornu-English is not without its problems, however. Historically, it has mainly been the form which has been associated with provincialism, with rurality, and, unlike the ambitions of Revived Cornish, often has a comedic edge, a self-deprecating ideology,[182] and perhaps in the contemporary world a poor sense of worth compared to the dialects within English across the isles of Britain.[183] Cornu-English has been in ascendance as a language since the decline of Cornish and

---

180. Penhallurick, op.cit. (2000).

181 See M. F. Wakelin, *Language and History in Cornwall* (Leicester, 1975); D. J. North, *Studies in Anglo-Cornish Phonology* ((Redruth, 1983); D. J. North and A. Sharpe, *A Word-Geography of Cornwall* (Redruth, 1980).

182 See some of the selections in Les Merton (ed.), *Thus Es Et: An Anthology of Cornish Dialect* (London, 2011).

183 Cf. say, Scotland, the North East of England, Essex or Liverpool. These are widely represented in the media.

there has been much discussion regarding linguistic links between Cornish and Cornu-English. The Cornish language movement has generally been dismissive of these links, although there are scholars who have a different view and argue that survivals in Cornu-English may well be a better route into Revived Cornish for learners.[184] Certainly some terminology—say, from fishing or mining—has very close links.[185]

The philosophy of Cornu-English use is complex. The debate over its use is often down to what sociolinguists might term "modality" and the ability or non-ability of speakers to code switch. In Cornwall, mainly amongst the older generation, there are some speakers of Cornu-English who will not or who are unable to code switch. Their use of Cornu-English is sometimes indicated by a kind of fatalistic philosophy—with phrases and concepts suiting their worldview.[186] This fatalism is not always present, but it is also indicated by a nascent humour and belief in the absurdity of life—in effect, an existentialist agenda. This agenda has perhaps been shaped by a very long period of social history in Cornwall in which outwardly not very much went right—indicators of this include the decline of traditional industries, ways of life, and the old favourite of Cornish philosophy—the growth of in-migration (a concept originally alluded to in Scawen).[187] It is as if, to use Payton's term, "historical experience" has created part of this existentialist ethics.[188] A number of texts embody this philosophical outlook, often attached directly to the working

184 Most famously argued by W. S. Lach-Szyrna. See Kent and Saunders (ed.), op.cit., pp. 323-6, and also opined by Henry Jenner. See various contributors to D. R. Williams (ed.), op.cit..

185 Embodied in R.M. Nance, *A Glossary of Cornish Sea Words* (Cornwall, 1963); W. G. Orchard, *A Glossary of Mining Terms* (Redruth, 1991).

186 Many of these are found in Phillipps, op.cit.

187 Payton, op.cit., (1993).

188 Payton, op.cit, (1992).

class of Cornwall. The early stories of Jack Clemo and the plays of Robert Morton Nance represent the highpoint of the genre.[189]

It is, however, a good deal more complex than this. There are a number of native Cornu-English speakers who know precisely the way to use this form of language, but are able to code-switch according to circumstance and community. Thus, clearly given Cornwall's accommodation, the business of society, education, medicine, and work is conducted in Standard English, yet upon discovery of other Cornu-English speakers, they can code switch and return to their most comfortable form of speaking. When it is clear that speakers either dominate or are in an exclusive group of Cornu-English speakers, then Cornu-English is used. A huge philosophical question is opened up by this phenomenon because we wonder why such natural speech has to be repressed within its native territory. We perhaps know some of the reasons for this: sometimes, because of the dominance of Standard English, speakers of Cornu-English feel socially uncomfortable. This is because there is huge pressure by media, society, and business to conform. As noted above, this phenomenon is not given sympathetic treatment by those concerned with Cornish. Indeed, the Standard English speakers paradoxically are often intrigued by the survival and retention of the Cornish language. In fact, the metropolitan centre and media finds it fascinating that Cornish and Cornishness have survived into the twenty-first century. Thus, Standard English speakers and some Cornish-language speakers collude in the repressing of Cornu-English.

---

189 J. Clemo, *The Bouncing Hills* (Redruth, 1983); R. M. Nance, *The Cledry Plays: Drolls of Old Cornwall for Village Acting and Home Reading* (Cornwall, 1956). See also the reflections of D. Philip, *No Times for Tears: Reflections of a Cornish Childhood* (Redruth, 1994).

Much is made by some organizations and individuals of the decline of Cornu-English. It may be the case that there is a decline in some terminology and popular use, and yet Cornu-English continues in routine use. Like all languages, it absorbs and adapts wider emergent concepts and drops others which are no longer required due to historical change. Thus, it is hard to see why many traditional mining terms or phrases would survive when little mining is taking place.[190] In essence, this is why it is important for film-makers, poets, writers, and musicians to re-engage with Cornu-English and to reinvigorate its importance in the philosophy of the Cornish mind. Perhaps in order to complete this, it has been necessary to merge and collate traditional sub-divisions of Cornu-English use.

There is also satire of the fatalistic use of Cornu-English as a marker of philosophy. The philosophical concept of "dreckly" is important to consider here. Dreckly, in this sense, means things get done when they get done, and not before. Cornish rappers Hedluv and Passman released a song titled "Dreckly" in 2011. Some of the lyrics of the song are:

> That's the way down 'ere, down
> We don't down much in a day down 'ere
> I can't get a job or get paid down'ere
> But there's nowhere to spend it anyway down 'ere
> That's ok down 'ere
> I walk through a lovely landscape down 'ere
> That's the pace down 'ere
> There's country lanes, no motorways down 'ere
> It takes as long as it takes down 'ere.[191]

---

190 See Orchard, op.cit.
191 See http://www.youtube.com/watch?v=IElsg1VOcVA. Accessed 25 April 2013. For another look at dreckly, see L. Merton, *Dreckly: A Collection of Possibilities* (Redruth, 2011).

Hedluv and Passman seem to be poking fun at the attitude in some Cornish people that is embodied in a fatalistic philosophy and a view that, despite modernity, there will be no change. However, within this sarcasm, we also note the economic concern over employment and that the Cornish landscape is still inspirational (in a sense not distant from what the visiting philosophers offered). What is intriguing about this satire on Cornish philosophy is that it is not too distant in its outlook from some of the nineteenth-century's Cornu-English poetry (where often the Cornish felt "innocent" abroad or "up the line") or even some poetry of the twentieth century.[192] This is even more ironic when one considers the philosophical energy of the Cornish overseas—both historically and in the present. In this we have another paradox—philosophically, the Cornish can acclimatize well to wherever they find themselves in the world, and yet with that is a kind self-reflection and uncertainty. In this sense, the world is "too big", "too un-Cornish" and the desire is to return to the peninsula. Such a philosophy is noted in much of the writings of the Cornish overseas.[193]

Of late, interest in Cornu-English has seen something of a revival. A generation of writers have embraced Cornu-English in new ways and have tried to express Cornish philosophy and ideology beyond fatalism and comedy.[194] Likewise, the value

---

192 See entries in Merton, op.cit.
193 Kent and McKinney. op.cit.
194 See, for example, A M. Kent, *Voodoo Pilchard* (Wellington, 2010): M. Combellack, *The Permanent History of Penaluna's Van* (Peterborough, 2003); N. R. Philips, *Rainbows in the Spray* (Redruth, 2012), D. R. Rawe, *Spargo's Confession* (Wadebridge, 2010); Craig Weaeherhill, *The Inner's Way* (Padstow, 2010). See various contributors to L. Merton (ed.) *Poetry Cornwall /Barthoyneth Kernow* (Redruth, 2007-2013) and A. M, Kent (ed.), *Four Modern Cornish Plays* (London, 2010). See also B. Harvey (dir,), *Weekend Retreat* (Truro, 2001).

TOWARDS A CORNISH PHILOSOPHY

and interest in Cornu-English has been brought to the fore by observers such as Ken Phillipps, Brian Stevens, and, more recently, Les Merton.[195] Anthologies have philosophically forced scholars, cultural gatekeepers, and the public to re-engage with Cornu-English.[196] The internet, too, has helped with preservation and compilation. Perhaps the biggest breakthrough with Cornu-English has been in the realm of social media. Such technology has permitted the speaking group to maintain its voice and cultural agenda. Commonly circulated images on Facebook are the posters "Cornish not English" and "Matter, do ut?",[197] but we can also find an adaptation of the now famous wartime advice: "Keep Calm me Ansum. I'll do it Dreckly".[198] The anonymity of Social Media and the friendship status of the group has facilitated new cultural exchanges. Entries and comments also see communicators much more willing to write in Cornu-English forms—again for humour, but also for social comment and cultural revival. There has also been a more aggressive marketing of Cornu-English as a marker of difference within the tourism industry. A popular souvenir is a list of Cornish Words and Phrases, creating humour and interest through the merging of language in Cornu-English, and by offering Standard English "translations". Here is a sample:

195   See Phillipps, op.cit; Brian Stevens helps coordinate Cornu-English entries for the Federations of Old Cornwall Societies. See http://www.cornishdialect.oldcornwall.org; L. Merton, *Cornish Dialect* (Sheffield, 2012).
196   Merton. op.cit. (2011).
197   "Cornish: Not English"—Steve Curgenven to Alan Kent 5 April 2013. "Matter do ee?"—Kayleigh Bray to Alan Kent 11 May 2013.
198   "Keep Calm Me Ansum. I'll do it dreckly"—James Lobb to Alan Kent 5 April 2013.

Aveedunun	Have you taken the necessary steps to complete the course of action?
Costymuchdida	Are you preparing to tell me how much it cost you?
Diddyadm	Did you have it? Did he/she have it? Did anyone have it?
Fariza	How far away is my destination?
Goynary	Are you proposing to go?[199]

Such fusions and interpretations of speech patterns in Cornu-English may, on the face of it, seem just as deprecating as earlier dialect narratives and poems, and yet there is both a truth of thought, logic, and language operating within them that do seem to express a genuine and tangible Cornish philosophy which may well be at the modern end of the philosophical characteristics first identified by Scawen and Elliot-Binns.

---

199 *Cornish Words and Phrases* List. Purchased in Perranporth, 2005.

11

The Philosophy of Stones

In the ground and in the mind: "Fake" Cromlechs and New Crosses

Whilst Cornish language and Cornu-English are central tenets of the philosophy of the Cornish, there is perhaps one more clearly identifiable aspect of Cornish life related to thought, logic, and ethics. We have already examined Cornwall's geography in helping to create indigenous philosophy, yet because of Cornwall's unique geological position, stone in all its forms and kinds, seems to be central in the Cornish mind.[200] Such awareness is embodied in the antiquarian writers of the past who, without modern archaeological methods, speculated on the links between the stone structures and remains, and the lives of the West Britons. Some went further and made direct links to an imagined druidic culture.[201] This, as we have seen, was embodied in the Romantic construction of Cornwall—in the writings of Le Grice and the poetry of Harris, for example.[202] Various travellers to Cornwall through the

---

200 R. Payne and R. Lewsey, *The Romance of Stones* (Fowey, 1999).

201 W. Borlase, *Antiquities Historical and Monumental of the County of Cornwall* (London, 1754); W. C. Borlase, *Nænia Cornubiæ: The Cromlechs and Tumuli of Cornwall* (Felinfach, 1994 [1972]). See also A. Walsham, *The Reformation of Landscape: Religion, Identity and Memory in Early Modern Britain and Ireland* (Oxford, 2012).

202 See J. Harris, *Luda: A Lay of the Druids* (London, 1868).

centuries have made much of the connection of the Cornish to stone structures,[203] and the link is further reinforced by connections in folklore and folktales.[204] There would seem to be, then, something in the Cornish mind and worldview which has a direct engagement with stone. Perhaps this has been born out of centuries of mining. Perhaps, too, the link was made in the older Cornish worldview that, after the Biblical flood, the world's mineral and stone resources were redistributed and deposited in Cornwall; hence the obsession in Cornish folklore with Noah and the Flood.[205] Certainly this link has continued in the modern era—witnessed in the visits of Colquhoun and Crowley, as well as the work of Michell.

The link continued both in the early development of Cornish Studies (not least because its principal initial architect was an archaeologist),[206] but also from the on-going obsession with the preservation of this material past of "stone". One sees this in pages of journals, in the development of heritage organizations and in the conflicts over heritage and identity.[207] Popularly, stone structures are also seen in many Cornish gardens and venues; they are used in tourist literature to promote Cornwall as a place of mystery and intrigue. There is a sub-genre of active writing devoted to such stones.[208] Therefore, they must be significant in Cornish philosophy and the Cornish mindset. To demonstrate this, I will now examine three contemporary examples.

---

203 See T. Gray (ed.), *Cornwall: The Traveller's Tales* (Exeter, 2000).
204 See Hunt, op.cit., Bottrell. op.cit.
205 See Kent and Saunders. op.cit., p.345. See also P. Neuss (ed. and tr.), *The Creacion of the World: A Critical Edition and Translation* (New York and London, 1983).
206 See Thomas. op.cit.
207 See *Cornish Archaeology / Hendyscans Kernow*; leaflet of the *Cornwall Heritage Trust.*; Angarrack, op.cit.
208 C. Weatherhill. *Cornovia: Ancient Sites of Cornwall and Scilly* (Penzance, 1985); Straffon, op.cit; Kent, op. cit. (2012).

Following the opening of the Dobwalls by-pass in 2008, the newly-constructed roundabout at the western end of the village remained undeveloped. However, in April 2013, the Highways Agency and Cornwall Council constructed an addition to the roundabout to make the location more attractive. It is interesting that the choice of structure made for this key roundabout is a destroyed or ruined cromlech or quoit.[209] Thus in the second decade of the twenty-first century, stone structures seem to offer both a vision of who the Cornish are as well as reinforcing their deep connection to stone. The structure mounted on the roundabout strongly echoes the nearby Trethevy Quoit (a Neolithic chamber tomb), but also recalls other iconic structures further to the west such as Zennor and Lanyon Quoits. Its mock ruination seem to contribute to both the sense of romanticism established by poets such as Le Grice and Harris, but also that wider philosophical outlook of lament and awareness of a lost past culture, destroyed by modernity. The erection of the new quoit at Dobwalls echoed the re-erection of another "real" quoit at Carwynnen near Troon in West Cornwall in the same period.[210]

Located on one of the major trunk roads into Cornwall, the structure at Dobwalls surely tells the visitor something of native philosophy and what it is about the Cornish that will survive. So important are such icons, that modern versions are created to both reinforce the older identity but also eek out permanence in the form of stone for the next few centuries. Perhaps such stone structures display a renewed confidence that paradoxically sits alongside the loss. Of course, modern engagement with stone structures is not new. One might argue

209   http://www.facebook.com/BBCRadioCornwall Accessed 25 April 2013.
210   See http://www.sustrust.co.uk/conservation.html. Accessed 25 April 2013.

that Barbara Hepworth had also completed such a project with her statues and carvings in the middle decades of the twentieth century (which were strongly influenced by Mên-an-tol and the menhirs of West Penwith),[211] and at the opposite end of Cornish culture, self-appointed Arch-Druid of Cornwall, Ed Prynne of St Merry also developed a number of imitations of famous structures in the garden of his bungalow.[212] Often dismissed as eccentric, Prynne's monuments strike at a philosophical engagement with stone that runs deep inside the Cornish.

In the same week that the quoit at Dobwalls was erected, a re-imagined version of another iconic Cornish structure was erected at Saltash. As part of a woodland regeneration scheme on the western bank of the River Tamar, close to the Tamar Bridge, a twenty-metre high carbon and resin cross was constructed. The cross is plated in gold, silver, and copper. Designed by artist Simon Thomas, the cross had originally been designed to celebrate the millennium but was eventually installed some thirteen years later. Joe Ellison, a Saltash town councillor and leader of the project was quoted on BBC Radio Cornwall as saying that the cross could become "Cornwall's equivalent of the Angel of the North".[213] The success of this project remains to be seen for it is significantly smaller than Antony Gormley's structure at Gateshead. However, like the quoit at Dobwalls, such a structure draws down on the philosophical associations that crosses of this kind are integral to a Cornish worldview. It is widely known that there are over

211 B. Hepworth, *Barbara Hepworth—A Pictorial Autobiography* (London, 1985).

212 R. Roy, *Stone Circles: A Modern Builder's Guide to the Megalithic Revival* (Totnes, 1999), pp.103-22.

213 See http://www.bbc.co.uk/news/uk-england-cornwall-19341692. Accessed 24 April http://www.sustrust.co.uk/conservation.html 2013.

four hundred such stone crosses in Cornwall, and that many were adaptations of pre-Christian menhirs.[214] Once again, the combination of Pagan and Christian seem integral to the understanding of self; enhanced in this case by the coating of mined metals. Here, the native philosophy seems to dovetail with that of visitors—as in the writings and observations of Colquhoun, Crowley, and Michell.

Incredibly, just as these two structures were erected, a third high profile news story examined a proposed housing development at Tregunnel in Newquay. Although debate over the need for new housing and an end to second home ownership continues, here the developers (the Duchy of Cornwall) boasted of the Cornishness of their project, explicitly stating that roofing tiles for the new dwellings would contain Cornish slate quarried from Trevillet near Tintagel.[215] This is in strong contrast to the normal ironic import of cheaper slate from overseas. One might question whether this was effectively a political and environmental sop to those who claim Cornwall does not need these new homes. However, it might also be part of a wider philosophical tide—connected to those wider issues of Conservative "localism" and, to an extent, Cornish self-determination. However, there is much contestation on this subject. The Duchy of Cornwall is owned as a business by the Prince of Wales and its operation is often criticized by Cornish activists.[216] Such a gesture by the Duchy of Cornwall again opens a philosophical debate over direction and place.

---

214 See A. Langdon, *Stone Crosses in West Penwith* (Cornwall, 1997). Further volumes deal with West Cornwall, East Cornwall, Mid Cornwall and North Cornwall.

215 See http://www.bbc.co.uk/news/uk-england-cornwall-22239938. Accessed 23 April 2013.

216 See http://www.cornishstannaryparliament.co.uk. Accessed 23 April 2013.

12

Philosophy or no?

The Timeless Land

Although perhaps seemingly tangential to our wider discussion of a native Cornish philosophy it does appear that stone and Cornish engagement with it, is one of the central components of our thought processes. Stone, in the form of geology, shapes Cornish peripherality and peninsularity. It also shapes the ritual and built environments and, as shown above, the imaginary conceptualization of "self". Stone takes a long time to erode. It is but one example of these key markers. It is part of what Denys Val Baker—always with an eye on the philosophical endeavour of the Cornish—labelled the "timeless land".[217] This is part of the issue: the philosophy of the Cornish goes back through time—to "time immemorial".[218] That is perhaps part of the obsession or connection with stone. With this in mind, it is then logical to posit other markers of the Cornish "worldview" which inform native philosophy. These might be indicators such as mining, fishing, and farming each with "states of mind" which are informed by tradition and culture, and which have evolved throughout Cornish history. Likewise particular moments in the ritual year (both Christian

---

217 D. Val Baker, *The Timeless Land: The creative spirit in Cornwall* (Bath, 1973).

218 See arguments in Harrison. op.cit.

71

and Pagan) have helped to reinforce a philosophy of Life.[219] These may be taken from as diverse areas as Methodism, Neo-festival culture, surfing, and social media.

This monograph has posited that Pengelly's "Cornish Paradox" is very much at the heart of Cornish philosophy for the West Britons at the start of the twentieth century. If we return to manuscript and literary sources, we note the emergence of a native Cornish philosophy which truly engaged with thought and language on a pan-European level. The paradox, as argued here, has shown that similar to the way the Cornish mind has to deal with nation-state and county, it has had to deal with the twin precepts of the Enlightenment and Romanticism. In this way, Cornish philosophy might be seen to be trapped or caught between two positions—and this might well have determined the Cornish sense of self for a very long time. Alternatively, this juxtaposition may need rethinking and working through in order for Cornishness to progress further in the current century and beyond. A key difficulty for the average Cornishman or woman is trying to maintain ethnic credibility without having to move into "nationalist" attack. This is another way of seeing the "Cornish Paradox". Yet all of this is indicative of wider negotiations the average Cornish person has to deal with. The negotiations are part of what makes a person Cornish.

Undoubtedly as we have additionally seen in this mono-graph, many Cornish people feel a spirituality or even a religiosity but it is very often caught between the Christian and Pagan, and the resultant Christian guilt that follows—as a residual element of previous social history and Christianized philosophy. As we move towards an even more secular world and one in Cornwall which has become more attentive to, and assertive of, its Pagan traditions, then we can expect to see

---

219 G. Tregidga (ed.), *Memory, Place and Landscape: The Cultural Landscapes of Cornwall* (London, 2012).

philosophical change far removed from the Christianized—Graeco-Roman traditions which have dominated for so long. In this transition, there is still much scholarship to be completed. As contributors to a recent volume have argued, the debate is being opened up about memory, place, and landscape, and, hopefully about philosophy too.[220]

In a text of this size and scope, I have tried to open a debate about the philosophy of the Cornish. It would have been impossible to have covered all the possible avenues of exploration, and yet my hope is that more scholars will pay attention to this issue in the future. There will be insights into Cornish philosophy that I have not yet considered, but which should be welcomed by anyone concerned with the position and status of the Cornish. We also need to examine "gendered" philosophies of Cornwall as well: how men and women respond to place and community in different ways. Cornish philosophy might actually begin to define itself if it could identify further examples of how the group, the society, and the individual are caught between poles of experience. Being Cornish might mean having to continually bang one's head against these alternative perspectives of being in the way that perhaps other Celtic groups and individuals do not have to do. This complexity of identity and worldview is, in this author's mind, approaching the truth about how the Cornish can truly see themselves. Cornish narrative perception of self (which, at the end of the day, all philosophy is about) is about walking a path between very distinctive differences that are encountered in the media, on the internet, in England (in particular), in world history, and perhaps even more incredibly, at home, in the streets of both Penzance or Launceston.

Matter, do ut? Yes. Actually, it does.

---

220 S. Reed, *The Cornish Traditional Year* (London, 2012).

Lightning Source UK Ltd.
Milton Keynes UK
UKOW04f1520031013

218385UK00001B/11/P